Brain Teasers for Team Leaders

Hundreds of Word Puzzles and Number Games to Energize Your Meetings

Leslie Bendaly

McGraw-Hill Ryerson

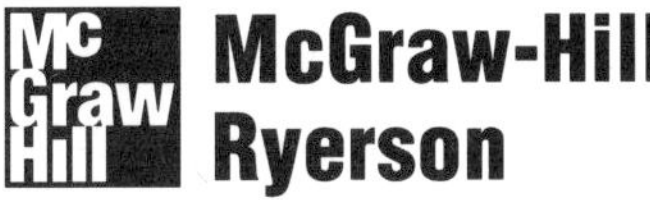

Toronto Montréal Burr Ridge, IL Dubuque, IA Madison, WI New York San Francisco St. Louis Bangkok Beijing Bogotá Caracas Kuala Lumpur Lisbon London Madrid Mexico City Milan New Delhi Santiago Seoul Singapore Sydney Taipei

McGraw-Hill
Ryerson Limited

A Subsidiary of The ***McGraw-Hill*** *Companies*

ISBN: 0-07-087398-4

1234567890 MP 01234567890
Printed and bound in Canada.

Canadian Cataloguing in Publication Data

Bendaly, Leslie
Brain teasers for team leaders: hundreds of word puzzles and number games to energize your meetings

ISBN 0-07-087398-4

1. Teams in the workplace. 2. Group games. I. Title.

HD66.B448 2000 658.3'128 C00-932010-5

Publisher: **Joan Homewood**
Editorial Co-ordinator: **Catherine Leek**
Production Co-ordinator: **Susanne Penny**
Electronic Page Composition: **Neda Hadjis**
Cover Design: **Sharon Lucas**

Table of Contents

Energize Your Meetings

Brainteasers challenge the intellect and add an element of fun to any meeting. I have coached corporate teams for 15 years and know that 10 minutes invested at the beginning of a meeting (or at selected intervals if the meeting is a full day one) pays a huge return. The energy level of the group, and the degree of participation and innovation have always determined the quality of a meeting's outcomes. Now in the 21st century as the pace of change continues to accelerate, competition grows fiercer and more and more decisions are being made and implemented by teams, those success ingredients are even more critical.

Introducing brainteasers can help you accomplish one or all of the following:

- Get people's minds into the meeting. Meeting members are often preoccupied with whatever they left behind when they entered the meeting room. Focusing on brainteasers forces them to set everything else aside.

- Spark creative thinking. We ask people to be creative and think outside of the box but often provide only a "box" like meeting and thinking environment—often the same meeting room, perhaps even the same place at the meeting table, a predictable agenda, the same tone/atmosphere.

Brainteasers change the tone of the meeting which in itself encourages different thinking. In addition, brainteasers demand that participants exercise a part of their brain that usually isn't tapped during traditional problem solving sessions. Studies have also shown that innovation is much more likely to emerge in an environment in which people are having fun.

- Increase participation. Brainteasers warm the group up. Meeting members generally find it easy and enjoyable to participate in a brainteaser activity and having found participating non threatening, in fact enjoyable, tend to continue in a heightened participatory mode once you move into the meeting agenda.

The one thousand and some brainteasers presented here have been organized for easy reproduction. You may choose to reproduce them on acetates or as handouts.

Tip: Breaking the group into smaller teams to solve the brainteasers and pitting the teams against one another can add an additional element of fun. It also encourages people to move into a "working together" mode.

If the meeting has a team-building element, solving a set of brainteasers as a team has an additional benefit. The advantages of working as a team are quickly apparent as each member brings their own particular perceptions, skills and experiences to the puzzle solving process.

Enjoy!

Visit Leslie's web site: www.lbendaly.com.

If you have brainteasers or other meeting warm ups that you would like to share with others please email them to Leslie at: lbendaly@istar.ca or mail them to: Ortran, 277 Oriole Parkway, Toronto, Ontario, M5P 2H4.

BRAIN TEASERS

CLUE

blflowersoom

Answer:

flowers in bloom

Brain Teaser #1

Find the expression or phrase that each of these represents.

CLUE

blflowersoom

Answer:

flowers in bloom

1.

tire

2.

Ph.d
B.A.
M.A.
———
o

3.

Lived
Lived ←

4.

LINE

5.

trooper trooper

6.

pastry

7.

ecaFFace

8.

d
n
u
o
ar

Brain Teaser #2

Find the expression or phrase that each of these represents.

CLUE

blflowersoom

Answer:

flowers in bloom

1.

N
E
T
H
G
I
L

2.

your rope being

3.

KCIUQ

4.

E
BUZZ M

5.

line
line
line←

6.

HURRICANE

7.

ha ir
ha ir
ha ir
ha ir

8.

rcatcherye

Brain Teaser #3

CLUE

blflowersoom

Answer:

flowers in bloom

Find the expression or phrase that each of these represents.

1.

NOAH

2.

dnose
e
n
r
u
t

3.

rung
rung
rung ←

4.

thought an

5.

t
h
g
i
a
r
t
s

6.

budget
———
enter

7.

wro
n
g

8.

N D
M I

Brain Teaser #4

Find the expression or phrase that each of these represents.

CLUE

blflowersoom

Answer:

flowers in bloom

1.

2.

h
deumps

3.

limit
u
o
y

4.

5.

Ja et
ck
Ja et
ck
Jacket ←

6.

start story

7.

8.

line get off

Brain Teaser #5

Find the expression or phrase that each of these represents.

CLUE

blflowersoom

Answer:

flowers in bloom

1. Space

2. E
I
EITIE

3. yourself yourself

4. t
r
a
t
s

5. obvious   looking

6. PAIR PAIR

7. tI toG eH

8. r
e
t
e
m
o
r
a
b

Brain Teaser #6

Find the expression or phrase that each of these represents.

CLUE

blflowersoom

Answer:
flowers in bloom

1.

Going
———
Board

2.

scope scope

3.

gpurrsulf

4.

5.

my mind

6.

warning warning
warning warning

7.

I'm
Ever

8.

circuit
circuit ←

Brain Teaser #7

Find the expression or phrase that each of these represents.

CLUE

blflowersoom

Answer:

flowers in bloom

1.

people

2.

p p
r r
e way
s s
s s

3.

bank

4.

stibasicnct

5.

hands

6.

living

7.

handed

8.

murder meditated

Brain Teaser #8

CLUE

blflowersoom

Answer:

flowers in bloom

Find the expression or phrase that each of these represents.

1. battle

2. she / world

3. link link link___ link link

4. gnillevarTravelling

5. cover / agent

6. w o r h t

7. rheed

8. joke / you

Brain Teaser #9

Find the expression or phrase that each of these represents.

CLUE

blflowersoom

Answer:

flowers in bloom

1.

bet
horse

2.

rodiamondugh

3.

t
e
k
m a r

4.

3 cents
\- 1 cent
2 cents

5.

exposure exposure

6.

s mmer

7.

golf

8.

4'
3'
2'
1' story

Brain Teaser #10

Find the expression or phrase that each of these represents.

CLUE

blflowersoom

Answer:

flowers in bloom

1.

P A I N S

2.

n ews

3.

jump

4.

Y
V
I

5.

blessed blessed

6.

return
investment

7.

thedriveater

8.

sand
sand
sand
sand
sand

Brain Teaser #11

Find the expression or phrase that each of these represents.

CLUE

blflowersoom

Answer:

flowers in bloom

1.

1. chance
2.
3. chance
4. chance

2.

DEhe**BT**

3.

cake
cake
cake

4.

times times *times*
times **times**
TIMES times

5.

once
---
time

6.

ti gnitteg

7.

Figure

8.

safe Sorry

Brain Teaser #12

Find the expression or phrase that each of these represents.

CLUE

blflowersoom

Answer:

flowers in bloom

1.

me it

2.

working
———
time

3.

phrase phrase

4.

5.

notch ←
notch
notch

6.

try try

7.

lunch, dinner, lunch, dinner

8.

castles

Brain Teaser #13

Find the expression or phrase that each of these represents.

CLUE

blflowersoom

Answer:

flowers in bloom

1.

Ti
e

2.

startstart

3.

vesmurdertigation

4.

SMOKE
SMOKE
SMOKE
SMOKE

5.

cONCERN

6.

practice
Practice
Practice
Practice

7.

b
u
t
t
o
n
collar

8.

all
———
board

Brain Teaser #14

Find the expression or phrase that each of these represents.

CLUE

blflowersoom

Answer:
flowers in bloom

1.

money money
money money money
money money money
money money money

2.

3.

trading

4.

mount mount importance

5.

6.

hsingarmony

7.

e
s
o
l
c

8.

ACT

Brain Teaser #15

Find the expression or phrase that each of these represents.

CLUE

blflowersoom

Answer:
flowers in bloom

1. STAKES

2. VIOLET

3. pressure / strong

4. dritawer
drawer
drawer
drawer

5. CHESS CHESS

6. deppils

7. o oooo o o o o o o o o
ooo o o dom o o o o o
oo o o o o o o o o o o o o o
o ooooo o o o o o o

8. hand
hand clothes
hand
hand

Brain Teaser #16

Find the expression or phrase that each of these represents.

CLUE

blflowersoom

Answer:

flowers in bloom

1.

question question
question question
question question

2.

STUFF

3.

water
exploration

4.

DEFICIT

5.

duck

6.

natfasion

7.

e
eye
e

8.

politically
politicely
politically ←

Brain Teaser #17

Find the expression or phrase that each of these represents.

CLUE

blflowersoom

Answer:

flowers in bloom

1.

woods woods woods
woods woods woods
woods cabin woods
woods woods woods

2.

t
h
g
u
o
r
Well b

3.

ONE

4.

nail
nail
nail
cofnailfin

5.

drug + ict

6.

sense, sense, sense
sense, sense, sense ←

7.

shoe shoe

8.

earned
———
he
———
spent

Brain Teaser #18

Find the expression or phrase that each of these represents.

CLUE

blflowersoom

Answer:

flowers in bloom

1\.

2\.

TOP

3\.

blfillank

4\.

medic medic

5\.

CAT CAT

6\.

performance performance

7\.

timetime

8\.

thought thought
thought
thought thought thought
thought thought
thought thought

Brain Teaser #19

Find the expression or phrase that each of these represents.

CLUE

blflowersoom

Answer:

flowers in bloom

1.

10 10 10 10 10
10 10 10 10
10 10 10 moment

2.

High way

3.

4.

confinement

5.

friendjustfriend

6.

evidence

7.

8.

she

---

reproach

Brain Teaser #20

Find the expression or phrase that each of these represents.

CLUE
blflowersoom
Answer: *flowers in bloom*

1.

silent, silent, silent,
silent, noisy, silent,
noisy, silent, silent,
silent, silent, silent

2.

n o i s i c e d

3.

She life

4.

5.

noid noid

6.

FIRE

7.

ECAF

8.

Brain Teaser #21

Find the expression or phrase that each of these represents.

> **CLUE**
>
> blflowersoom
>
> Answer:
>
> *flowers in bloom*

1.

callcallcall

2.

MAIL

3.

C
U
T

4.

c
l
a
m
p

it

5.

message message message MESSAGE message

6.

it
MY TONGUE

7.

Ranger

8.

Brain Teaser #22

CLUE

blflowersoom

Answer:

flowers in bloom

Find the expression or phrase that each of these represents.

1.

H
e

2.

WOMEN HE

3.

go go go go go go

4.

mih to the law

5.

e
v
i
g

6.

7.

SAIL SAIL

8.

linereadline

Brain Teaser #23

Find the expression or phrase that each of these represents.

CLUE

blflowersoom

Answer:

flowers in bloom

1.

c l o w
e n i r

2.

fenalty

3.

BELIEF IT

4.

jobhejob

5.

ba ck work

6.

eggs
easy

7.

l
a
lmove

8.

d
e
f

Brain Teaser #24

Find the expression or phrase that each of these represents.

CLUE

blflowersoom

Answer:

flowers in bloom

1\.

crowd he

2\.

crSHEowd

3\.

place **place**
place place

4\.

ra
nk

5\.

a d v i c e

6\.

hooligan, hooligan,
hooligan, hooligan,
hooligan, hooligan,
hooligan, hooligan

7\.

he
———
suspicion

8\.

Mountain

Brain Teaser #25

Find the expression or phrase that each of these represents.

CLUE

blflowersoom

Answer:

flowers in bloom

1.

2.

it

3.

c
o
m
e
earth

4.

man man man man man
man giant man man man
man man man man man
man man man man man

5.

6.

Cake

7.

EYE

8.

redro

Brain Teaser #26

CLUE
blflowersoom

Answer:
flowers in bloom

Find the expression or phrase that each of these represents.

1.

LATE
Never

2.

KCAP

3.

B
R
E
A
K

4.

stand
~~leg~~

5.

crdiamondown

6.

day day day

7.

LOY ALTIES

8.

I'm

Brain Teaser #27

CLUE
blflowersoom

Answer:
flowers in bloom

Find the expression or phrase that each of these represents.

1.

idiot idiot idiot
idiot idiot idiot
idiot idiot idiot

2.

themfrictionthem

3.

4.

fight
—
money

5.

alkneesligators
e
h

6.

7.

Making IT

8.

pie pie pie
pie pie fingers pie pie
pie pie pie

Brain Teaser #28

Find the expression or phrase that each of these represents.

CLUE
blflowersoom

Answer:
flowers in bloom

1.

M
a
r
k
e
d

2.

YAP

3.

sinoendght

4.

play it play it

5.

MAST

6.

7.

leaf leaf leaf
leaf leaf leaf
leaf leaf leaf book
leaf leaf leaf

8.

trip
ccccc

Brain Teaser #29

CLUE
blflowersoom

Answer:
flowers in bloom

Find the expression or phrase that each of these represents.

1.

perspective *perspective*
perspective perspective

2.

3.

AR ROW

4.

e
k
a
m

5.

chicken

6.

roses roses roses roses
roses roses roses
roses roses roses roses

7.

TUNNEL light

8.

Opinion

Brain Teaser #30

CLUE
blflowersoom

Answer:
flowers in bloom

Find the expression or phrase that each of these represents.

1.

mansion mansion mansion
mansion mansion mansion
mansion mansion mansion
mansion mansion mansion

2.

Hill

3.

friends

4.

Let's m a k e

5.

Your money
Your money

6.

debeingpendent

7.

fire candle fire

8.

head
———
collision

Brain Teaser #31

Find the expression or phrase that each of these represents.

CLUE
blflowersoom

Answer:
flowers in bloom

1\.

Point of view. Point of view. Point of view. Point of view. Point of view. Point of view. Point of view. Point of view. Point of view. Point of view. Point of view. Point of view. Point of view. Point of view.

2\.

w e e k e n d

3\.

bitag

4\.

carpet

5\.

Think it Think

6\.

stomach EYES

7\.

ground
economy

8\.

gniog

Brain Teaser #32

CLUE
blflowersoom

Answer:
flowers in bloom

Find the expression or phrase that each of these represents.

1.

wake call

2.

3.

handed
———
he

4.

E A
L T H

5.

surcarance

6.

BROKE

7.

BUS
BUS

8.

bshipottle

Brain Teaser #33

CLUE
blflowersoom

Answer:
flowers in bloom

Find the expression or phrase that each of these represents.

1.

L
O
A
D

2.

cut cut cut

3.

pawalkrk

4.

kno wledge

5.

thug thug thug
thug thug thug
thug thug thug

6.

CO
A
Y

7.

ƐDGƐ

8.

Truth
Fiction

Brain Teaser #34

CLUE
blflowersoom

Answer:
flowers in bloom

Find the expression or phrase that each of these represents.

1. puFROGddle

2. bogeniettle

3. Dutch
Dutch

4. klaw

5. bet
———
it

6. flowers, flowers, flowers,
flowers, flowers, flowers,
flowers, flowers, flowers,
flowers, flowers, flowers

7. HOLE

8. e l i l l a g

Brain Teaser #35

CLUE
blflowersoom

Answer:
flowers in bloom

Find the expression or phrase that each of these represents.

1.

walking
ice

2.

call call call call

3.

ovnewation

4.

HAIR

5.

6.

vision vision

7.

too much
spending

8.

hittinghome

Brain Teaser #36

CLUE
blflowersoom

Answer:
flowers in bloom

Find the expression or phrase that each of these represents.

1. PAPER

2. straw
straw
straw
straw

3. all keyed

4. t
u
r
economy

5. header header

6. his peak performing

7. STARTING OUT

8. clean
clean
clean
clean

Brain Teaser #37

CLUE
blflowersoom

Answer:
flowers in bloom

Find the expression or phrase that each of these represents.

1\.

harm – fun =

2\.

decexposureent

3\.

niatruc

4\.

regret regret regret regret
regret regret regret regret
regret regret regret regret
regret regret regret regret

5\.

belt
―――――
hitting

6\.

a point
agree

7\.

8\.

Poor xqqqq

Brain Teaser #38

CLUE
blflowersoom

Answer:
flowers in bloom

Find the expression or phrase that each of these represents.

1.

garment
―――――
silk

2.

haneedleystack

3.

gone gone gone
gone conclusion

4.

go go
it it

5.

jumping 2 end
end end end

6.

BrIdGe

7.

repair it /
S

8.

foheg

Brain Teaser #39

CLUE
blflowersoom

Answer:
flowers in bloom

Find the expression or phrase that each of these represents.

1.

stand
---
try 2

2.

I'm unf lfilled

3.

corn
e
r

4.

warned warned
warned warned

5.

emotion EMOTION
Emotion emotion
emotion Emotion

6.

Metal

7.

the rewed

8.

sudden death
---
time

Brain Teaser #40

CLUE
blflowersoom

Answer:
flowers in bloom

Find the expression or phrase that each of these represents.

1.

t
n
u
o
c
c
account

2.

e
n
i
l

3.

bnƎ End

4.

n
o
i
t
a
l
f
n
i

5.

6.

formmisation

7.

it	it	
again		again

8.

Brain Teaser #41

Find the expression or phrase that each of these represents.

CLUE
blflowersoom

Answer:
flowers in bloom

1.

agreement

2.

engine engine

3.

MOOD

4.

llastine

5.

BLOOD
H2O

6.

Sailing
CCCC

7.

live
―――――
street

8.

another one

Brain Teaser #42

Find the expression or phrase that each of these represents.

> **CLUE**
> blflowersoom
>
> Answer:
> *flowers in bloom*

1.

2.

S
U
N

3.

4.

5.

6.

faslapce

7.

smuggling

---

border

8.

Brain Teaser #43

CLUE
blflowersoom

Answer:
flowers in bloom

Find the expression or phrase that each of these represents.

1.

line get to

2.

cast
cast
cast
cast

3.

WA**O**LL

4.

s
u
n

5.

hea
rt

6.

ban ana

7.

crying
———
spilled milk

8.

siendght

Brain Teaser #44

Find the expression or phrase that each of these represents.

CLUE
blflowersoom

Answer:
flowers in bloom

1.

e
t
n
a

2.

pepoisn ABCD
EFGH
IJKL

3.

MEMORY

4.

take take

5.

coulessonrage

6.

v a e s
g b e
l t e

7.

cottagesea

8.

answer
answer
answer

Brain Teaser #45

CLUE
blflowersoom

Answer:
flowers in bloom

Find the expression or phrase that each of these represents.

1.

achiever
———
he's an

2.

d i v i s i o n

3.

will will will [will] & bible

4.

demx2nity

5.

think
think think
think think

6.

way
way

7.

knheow

8.

d r a y

Brain Teaser #46

CLUE
blflowersoom

Answer:
flowers in bloom

Find the expression or phrase that each of these represents.

1.

cover
―――
cop

2.

3.

junk
junk
junk

4.

fosinglewomanrmation

5.

flame flame flame
flame g flame
o
flame

6.

Romeo & Juliet
―――
words

7.

men men men men
men man men men
men men men men

8.

stmishatements

CLUE
blflowersoom

Answer:
flowers in bloom

Find the expression or phrase that each of these represents.

1.

getting better getting better
getting better getting better

2.

quality quality
quality quality

3.

chute chute

4.

+ or -

5.

turn
—————
ten cents

6.

View

7.

popigke

8.

millionaire millionaire
millionaire millionaire
millionaire
millionaire millionaire
millionaire

Brain Teaser #48

CLUE
blflowersoom

Answer:
flowers in bloom

Find the expression or phrase that each of these represents.

1.

my words✓

2.

mapathnger

3.

it
u
r

4.

Symphon

5.

SECRETS

6.

7.

home   run

8.

his day 1 his day 2
his day 3 his day 4
his day 5

Brain Teaser #49

CLUE
blflowersoom

Answer:
flowers in bloom

Find the expression or phrase that each of these represents.

1.

2.

EG
G

3.

memories

4.

l i b e
g s
s n
s

5.

WAY HOUSE

6.

millchanceion

7.

pr4ess

8.

getting
it

Brain Teaser #50

CLUE
blflowersoom

Answer:
flowers in bloom

Find the expression or phrase that each of these represents.

1. skpiey

2. normal normal

3. **Leaf Leaf Leaf**
   Leaf ʇɐǝ˥

4. ne ck speed

5. **account**
   ―――――
   drawn

6. u
   pict res

7. job he job

8. 

Brain Teaser #51

Find the expression or phrase that each of these represents.

CLUE
blflowersoom

Answer:
flowers in bloom

1. sun sun

2. sislandun

3. feeling / world

4. nalp

5. Stor

6. world

7. pressed

8. question

Brain Teaser #52

CLUE
blflowersoom

Answer:
flowers in bloom

Find the expression or phrase that each of these represents.

1.

stood
young lady

2.

mymmyheartouth

3.

perfect perfect

4.

DO
W
N

5.

everything

6.

he art

7.

grate grate grate
grate grate
grate grate grate
grate grate

8.

Texas Texas
Texas Texas
Maine Maine
Maine Maine

Brain Teaser #53

CLUE
blflowersoom

Answer:
flowers in bloom

Find the expression or phrase that each of these represents.

1.

poppd

2.

splostace

3.

+ vance
―――――
green

4.

instant
instant

5.

You
t
i

6.

sisomso

7.

n n n n n
n n n m n n nnnn
nnnn n n n
n n nn nnnn nnn

8.

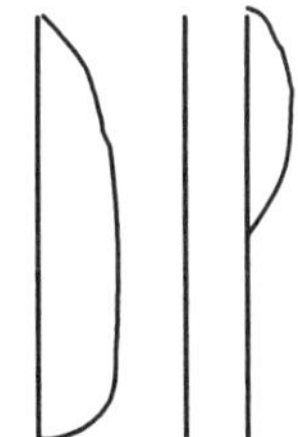

Brain Teaser #54

CLUE
blflowersoom

Answer:
flowers in bloom

Find the expression or phrase that each of these represents.

1.

ddeeplyebt

2.

$$\frac{\text{fire}}{\text{cool}}$$

3.

judgment
judgment
judgment ←

4.

FINGER

5.

going it

6.

time X 2

7.

ɘbiƨ

8.

Nerve
Nerve

Brain Teaser #55

CLUE
blflowersoom

Answer:
flowers in bloom

Find the expression or phrase that each of these represents.

1.

excforhange

2.

3.

engine engine

4.

5.

6.

icing
———
cake

7.

8.

fender

WHAT A DIFFERENCE A LETTER MAKES

CLUE
scar
lag
rile

Answer: ***f***
*scar**f***
***f**lag*
*ri**f**le*

What a Difference a Letter Makes #1

Find one letter that can be added to each of the three words to make a new word. The letter may be added to the beginning, end or within the word.

CLUE
scar
lag
rile

Answer: *f*
scarf
flag
rifle

1.

hat
ear
rail

2.

rum
ate
ill

3.

ray
wig
rip

4.

ridge
bar
race

5.

ice
are
tape

6.

ride
ace
age

7.

sake
ever
keel

8.

gape
asp
tee

What a Difference a Letter Makes #2

CLUE
scar
lag
rile

Answer: ***f***
*scar**f***
***f**lag*
*ri**f**le*

Find one letter that can be added to each of the three words to make a new word. The letter may be added to the beginning, end or within the word.

1.

rave
host
ape

2.

cape
bow
tam

3.

rade
error
able

4.

mid
ail
sad

5.

live
gate
bush

6.

pay
bow
tack

7.

ease
pay
it

8.

tale
ask
owl

What a Difference a Letter Makes #3

CLUE
scar
lag
rile

Answer: ***f***
*scar**f***
***f**lag*
*ri**f**le*

Find one letter that can be added to each of the three words to make a new word. The letter may be added to the beginning, end or within the word.

1.

save
air
sift

2.

late
low
pat

3.

air
sear
sow

4.

lice
lip
rap

5.

raft
lie
ramp

6.

lass
olden
amble

7.

wok
wing
ink

8.

hair
up
able

What a Difference a Letter Makes #4

Find one letter that can be added to each of the three words to make a new word. The letter may be added to the beginning, end or within the word.

CLUE
scar
lag
rile

Answer: ***f***
scarf
flag
rifle

1.

ale
rush
rim

2.

goat
side
paid

3.

gave
bead
tickle

4.

gavel
save
tack

5.

cave
elated
cove

6.

tap
after
cape

7.

ear
ever
use

8.

lass
as
litter

What a Difference a Letter Makes #5

CLUE
scar
lag
rile

Answer: ***f***
scarf
flag
rifle

Find one letter that can be added to each of the three words to make a new word. The letter may be added to the beginning, end or within the word.

1.

round
maze
glen

2.

ear
ram
ace

3.

dive
cap
aft

4.

own
rind
bare

5.

cat
ate
cart

6.

pay
adder
back

7.

all
hip
itch

8.

rip
rough
wig

What a Difference a Letter Makes #6

CLUE
scar
lag
rile

Answer: *f*
scarf
flag
rifle

Find one letter that can be added to each of the three words to make a new word. The letter may be added to the beginning, end or within the word.

1.

hip
have
lick

2.

fame
bought
gate

3.

food
imp
save

4.

seat
aft
ax

5.

after
tack
gain

6.

sake
at
sip

7.

gable
aim
ass

8.

pate
save
ever

What a Difference a Letter Makes #7

CLUE
scar
lag
rile

Answer: *f*
scarf
flag
rifle

Find one letter that can be added to each of the three words to make a new word. The letter may be added to the beginning, end or within the word.

1.

pot
lap
as

2.

hoe
oak
poke

3.

right
lack
rag

4.

beak
aft
tick

5.

ramp
ask
rim

6.

pan
ramp
ease

7.

liver
lick
upper

8.

lame
rave
rim

What a Difference a Letter Makes #8

CLUE
scar
lag
rile

Answer: ***f***
*scar**f***
***f**lag*
*ri**f**le*

Find one letter that can be added to each of the three words to make a new word. The letter may be added to the beginning, end or within the word.

1.

pace
pal
can

2.

lie
ramp
lip

3.

mile
word
mat

4.

ice
bag
fame

5.

rush
ash
pat

6.

kin
ample
lumber

7.

ale
ear
row

8.

air
camp
ill

What a Difference a Letter Makes #9

CLUE
scar
lag
rile

Answer: ***f***
*scar**f***
***f**lag*
*ri**f**le*

Find one letter that can be added to each of the three words to make a new word. The letter may be added to the beginning, end or within the word.

1.

rat
lower
lock

2.

rattle
lump
ram

3.

cat
pit
clap

4.

heat
gape
ace

5.

bake
cape
bead

6.

pat
hair
limb

7.

lass
rub
ripe

8.

ale
ill
utter

What a Difference a Letter Makes #10

CLUE
scar
lag
rile

Answer: ***f***
*scar**f***
***f**lag*
*ri**f**le*

Find one letter that can be added to each of the three words to make a new word. The letter may be added to the beginning, end or within the word.

1.
bust
bush
elated

2.
tier
old
as

3.
able
ale
otter

4.
late
ride
lug

5.
super
ass
out

6.
put
rust
ear

7.
boot
sake
cat

8.
pike
pout
hip

What a Difference a Letter Makes #11

Find one letter that can be added to each of the three words to make a new word. The letter may be added to the beginning, end or within the word.

CLUE
scar
lag
rile

Answer: f
scarf
flag
rifle

1.

tone
pace
tar

2.

for
pond
pot

3.

tin
air
tick

4.

lie
ail
may

5.

aster
rap
tie

6.

mid
know
put

7.

bind
ease
pay

8.

sad
gong
pant

SOMETHING IN COMMON

CLUE

Napkin
Nose
Circus

Answer:

ring

Something in Common #1

What do each of these words have in common.

CLUE

Napkin
Nose
Circus

Answer:
ring

1.
Shoe
Apple
Stone

2.
Mountain
Body
Ladder

3.
Leak
Product
Sink

4.
Back
Furniture
Race

5.
Goal
Letter
Sign

6.
Top
Web
Tale

7.
Ivy
Mountain
Social

8.
Directors
Room
Bulletin

Something in Common #2

What do each of these words have in common.

CLUE

Napkin
Nose
Circus

Answer:

ring

1.
Bermuda
Love
Isosceles

2.
Gravestone
Pill
Writing

3.
Work
Dead
Water

4.
Cement
Drink
Rain

5.
Hair
Gun
Straight

6.
Dog
Girl
Tour

7.
Coffee
Estate
Divorce

8.
Chocolate
Soap
Gold

Something in Common #3

What do each of these words have in common.

CLUE

Napkin
Nose
Circus

Answer:
ring

1.
Envelope
Crack
Lips

2.
Chocolate
Poker
Potato

3.
Traffic
Theatre
Plane

4.
Boat
Door
Hair

5.
Trunk
Dishwasher
Gun

6.
Tractor
Movie
Park

7.
Pencil
Camera
Detective

8.
Laundry
Collector
Machine

Something in Common #4

What do each of these words have in common.

CLUE

Napkin
Nose
Circus

Answer:
ring

1.
Basketball
Hockey
Fish

2.
Food
Cars
Friends

3.
Fishing
Story
Pencil

4.
Admirer
Code
Password

5.
Wall
Crepe
Writing

6.
School
Rope
Breakfast

7.
Movies
Partner
Night

8.
Cat
Phone
Curtain

Something in Common #5

What do each of these words have in common.

CLUE

Napkin
Nose
Circus

Answer:
ring

1.
Rooster
Ice cream
Head

2.
Dog
Band
Team

3.
Cup
Clip
Airplane

4.
Pedestrian
River
Cattle

5.
Surface
Tire
Landscape

6.
Christmas
Bingo
Score

7.
Bull
Criminal
Card

8.
Shopping
Cosmetic
Gym

Something in Common #6

What do each of these words have in common.

CLUE

Napkin
Nose
Circus

Answer:
ring

1.
Cake
Changed
Lived

2.
Toilet paper
Rock
Dinner

3.
Meter
Newspaper
Mind

4.
Tea
Saddle
Book

5.
Picture
Door
Car

6.
Table
Jell-O
Radio

7.
Envelope
Parachute
Bottle

8.
Sign
Letter
Score

Something in Common #7

What do each of these words have in common.

CLUE

Napkin
Nose
Circus

Answer:
ring

1.
Stamp
Hockey
Popsicle

2.
Paper
Cabbage
Evidence

3.
Liquor
Gun
Camera

4.
Corn
Soda
Gum

5.
Groceries
Rat
Suitcase

6.
Road
Utensil
Tree

7.
Card
Bull
Crime

8.
Fish
Door
Crochet

Something in Common #8

What do each of these words have in common.

CLUE

Napkin
Nose
Circus

Answer:
ring

1. Blade
Light
Railway tracks

2. Fishing
Car
Dog

3. Pig
Fountain
Play

4. Cake
Budget
Noise

5. Cherries
Winner
Ice

6. Plant
Band
Trees

7. Squares
Rendezvous
Calendar

8. Tree
Pack
Elephant

Something in Common #9

What do each of these words have in common.

CLUE

Napkin
Nose
Circus

Answer:
ring

1.
Lips
Money
Prize

2.
Book
Table
Tree

3.
Bottle
River
Face

4.
Cut
Stop
Circuit

5.
Memory
Blackboard
Tape

6.
Tie
Arrow
Gift

7.
Baseball
Bottle
Gun

8.
Fish
Peanut
Gun

Something in Common #10

What do each of these words have in common.

CLUE

Napkin
Nose
Circus

Answer:

ring

1. Plane
Face
Dive

2. Sugar
Rose
Punch

3. Time
Money
Energy

4. Mind
Edge
Dresser

5. Race
Business
Meeting

6. Fruit
Boxing
Paper

7. Salt
Dice
Head

8. Bank
Tree
River

Something in Common #11

What do each of these words have in common.

CLUE

Napkin
Nose
Circus

Answer:

ring

1. Bus
   Office
   Your life

2. Nails
   Picture
   Town

3. Clothes
   Hair
   Paint

4. Nails
   Documents
   Claim

5. Pennies
   Bottom
   Salt

6. Cherry
   Stomach
   Coal

7. Budget
   Scales
   Beam

8. Marathon
   Errand
   Temperature

Something in Common #12

What do each of these words have in common.

CLUE

Napkin
Nose
Circus

Answer:
ring

1. Boat
Book
Career

2. Load
Goose
Hen

3. Channels
Babies
Your mind

4. Risk
Temperature
Turn

5. Elevator
Arrow
Mine

6. Pen
Snake
Arrow

7. A drunk
Shoes
Collar

8. Rules
Spoon
Wire

Something in Common #13

What do each of these words have in common.

CLUE

Napkin
Nose
Circus

Answer:
ring

1.
Gears
Clothes
Mind

2.
Twig
Picture
Fingers

3.
Letter
Tomb
Deal

4.
Stamps
Pig
Tape

5.
Coin
Pancakes
Lid

6.
Eyes
Back
Tracks

7.
Rope
School
Breakfast

8.
Gun
Clothes
Ice

Something in Common #14

What do each of these words have in common.

CLUE

Napkin
Nose
Circus

Answer:
ring

1.
Lies
Cigarettes
Ice

2.
Flowers
Ice
Winner

3.
Bridge
Fishing nets
Clothes

4.
Ribbon
Losses
Finger

5.
CD
Game
Piano

6.
Bridges
Houses
Hopes

7.
Spirits
Children
Barns

8.
Glasses
Promises
The Law

Something in Common #15

What do each of these words have in common.

CLUE

Napkin
Nose
Circus

Answer:
ring

1.
A sign
A newspaper
A person

2.
The rules
Master
Parents

3.
Stamps
Coins
Cards

4.
Expectations
Agreement
Reputation

5.
Jury
Chair
Secret

6.
Dart
Stone
Party

7.
Door
Letter
Bottle

8.
Niche
Roast
Statue

Something in Common #16

What do each of these words have in common.

CLUE

Napkin
Nose
Circus

Answer:

ring

1.
Car
Game
Hair

2.
Exam
Gravy
Inspection

3.
Music
Note
Instructions

4.
Swings
Team
Stage

5.
Wind
Money
Bubble

6.
Grass
Finger
Classes

7.
Task
Police
Undue

8.
Letter
Window
Subject

Something in Common #17

What do each of these words have in common.

CLUE

Napkin
Nose
Circus

Answer:
ring

1.
Mind
Subject
Door

2.
Points
Beard
Wood

3.
Eggs
Rugs
Traffic

4.
Vow
Dinner
Joke

5.
Line
Ink
Mending

6.
Cards
Laundry
Newspaper

7.
Tantrum
Dice
Ball

8.
A picture
Your temperature
A chance

Something in Common #18

What do each of these words have in common.

CLUE

Napkin
Nose
Circus

Answer:

ring

1.
Fire
War
Car

2.
Hands
A club
Table

3.
Eye
Bottle
Season

4.
Late
Variety
Live

5.
Mountain
Big
Toy

6.
Glue
Toy
Shot

7.
Feet
Soul
Skin

8.
Dog
Package
Business deal

Something in Common #19

What do each of these words have in common.

CLUE

Napkin
Nose
Circus

Answer:

ring

1.
Career
Garden
Wrong

2.
Door
Indicator
Chain

3.
Door
Sign
Gap

4.
Chicken
Hydro
Hanger

5.
Neon
Astrological
Stop

6.
Rain
Snow
Hiking

7.
Chase
Bag
News

8.
Yo-yo
Pearls
Violin

Something in Common #20

What do each of these words have in common.

CLUE

Napkin
Nose
Circus

Answer:

ring

1.
Strap
Boot
Case

2.
Door
Cow
School

3.
Fast
Junk
Gourmet

4.
Brass
Tree
Mountain

5.
Button
Cart
Over

6.
Soap
Gun
Face

7.
Flakes
Fall
Ball

8.
Hockey
Broom
Gum

Something in Common #21

What do each of these words have in common.

CLUE

Napkin
Nose
Circus

Answer:

ring

1.
Man
Mat
Berry

2.
Bottle
Baseball
Pen

3.
Plug
Cart
Leg

4.
Grape
Money
Mustard

5.
Shoe
Silver
Apple

6.
Sweater
River
Bottle

7.
Party
Ball
Tantrum

8.
Bubble
Fuse
Glass

Something in Common #22

What do each of these words have in common.

CLUE

Napkin
Nose
Circus

Answer:

ring

1.
Neck
Promise
Glass

2.
Boy
Pipe
Bucket

3.
Water
Dream
Tobacco

4.
Phone
Bank
Match

5.
Mark
Case
Cover

6.
City
Universe
Chocolates

7.
Ship
Pole
Stone

8.
Hop
Bottom
Pepper

Something in Common #23

What do each of these words have in common.

CLUE

Napkin
Nose
Circus

Answer:

ring

1.
Upper
Bread
Pie

2.
Car
Robin
Jacket

3.
Arm
Box
Argument

4.
Rope
Breakfast
Town

5.
Fork
Sales
Baseball

6.
Hair
Grass
Losses

7.
Top
Garbage bag
Dance

8.
Paper
Beach
Man

Something in Common #24

What do each of these words have in common.

CLUE

Napkin
Nose
Circus

Answer:

ring

1.
Shoes
Car
Gems

2.
Picture
Twig
Fingers

3.
Arms
Heart
Fingers

4.
Garden
Bottom
Pile

5.
Button
Mouse
Sink

6.
A heart
A record
A glass

7.
Tire
Diaper
Clothes

8.
Thief
A cold
Butterfly

Something in Common #25

What do each of these words have in common.

CLUE

Napkin
Nose
Circus

Answer:
ring

1.
Ski
North
Jump

2.
French
Double
Fire

3.
Antiques
Coins
Stamps

4.
Cloud
Bed
Book

5.
Bed
Book
Barbeque

6.
Hair
Rug
Engine

7.
Clothes
Money
Mind

8.
Piano
Bar
Kitchen

Something in Common #26

What do each of these words have in common.

CLUE

Napkin
Nose
Circus

Answer:

ring

1. Floor
   Car
   Candle

2. Brief
   Camera
   Cosmetic

3. Paper
   Report
   Stand

4. Record
   Clock
   Example

5. Sign
   Watch
   Gap

6. Post
   Stop
   Astrological

7. Time
   Excuse
   Rib

8. Ski
   Straw
   Flag

Something in Common #27

What do each of these words have in common.

CLUE

Napkin
Nose
Circus

Answer:
ring

1.
Fly
Door
Mouse

2.
Lash
Glass
Private

3.
Horse
Ballet
Snow

4.
Dinner
Fashion
License

5.
Parcel
Office
Lamp

6.
Short
Hair
Rough

7.
Dinner
Lunch
Coffee

8.
Match
Cardboard
Jewelry

Something in Common #28

What do each of these words have in common.

CLUE

Napkin
Nose
Circus

Answer:

ring

1.
Collar
Stray
House

2.
Book
Sport
Straight

3.
Band
Knuckles
Buttons

4.
Carbon
News
Looseleaf

5.
Spin
Dog
Mountain

6.
Clock
Cloth
Powder

7.
Hall
Hockey
Swimming

8.
Post
Milk
Delivery

A NUMBER OF THINGS

CLUE

3 s and y o

Answer:
3 strikes and you're out

A Number of Things #1

Identify the expression, phrase or fact that is represented by each of the following combination of numbers and letters.

CLUE

3 s and y o

Answer:
3 strikes and you're out

1.

13 is a b d

2.

7 is a l n

3.

6 is a p of b

4.

45 d in a r a

5.

2 p in a q

6.

3 t in a t

7.

5 l p went to m

8.

12 i in a f

A Number of Things #2

CLUE

3 s and y o

Answer:
3 strikes and you're out

Identify the expression, phrase or fact that is represented by each of the following combination of numbers and letters.

1. 3 b m

2. 10 d in a d

3. 76 t

4. 12 m in a y

5. 29 d in f in a l y

6. 4 b on a b d

7. 2 to t

8. 7 w of the w

A Number of Things #3

Identify the expression, phrase or fact that is represented by each of the following combination of numbers and letters.

CLUE

3 s and y o

Answer:
3 strikes and you're out

1. 7 d of s w

2. 3 M

3. 10 is B D s

4. 26 l in the a

5. 52 c in a d

6. 2 s in a p

7. 2 h on a c

8. 12 d of C

A Number of Things #4

Identify the expression, phrase or fact that is represented by each of the following combination of numbers and letters.

CLUE

3 s and y o

Answer:
3 strikes and you're out

1. 100 c in a d

2. 7 d s

3. 8 s in a m p

4. 12 d of J

5. 5 c in a n

6. 3 r c

7. 3 f in a y

8. 24 c in a c

A Number of Things #5

Identify the expression, phrase or fact that is represented by each of the following combination of numbers and letters.

CLUE

3 s and y o

Answer:
3 strikes and you're out

1. 2 w on a b

2. 2 p in a p

3. 4 p on a f

4. 2 p in a p of t

5. 3 r b

6. 4 q in a w

7. 2 b in a s g

8. 4 l c

A Number of Things #6

Identify the expression, phrase or fact that is represented by each of the following combination of numbers and letters.

CLUE

3 s and y o

Answer:
3 strikes and you're out

1. 2 s to a c

2. 8 o in a h p

3. 1 p in a p t

4. 4 l h

5. 40 d in the d

6. 26 m in a m

7. 4 s in a d of c

8. 10 d in a d

A Number of Things #7

Identify the expression, phrase or fact that is represented by each of the following combination of numbers and letters.

CLUE

3 s and y o

Answer:
3 strikes and you're out

1. 12 m in the d d

2. 9 i in a b g

3. 12 m on a j

4. 1 e C

5. 12 s of the z

6. 9 l of a c

7. 4 q in a d of c

8. 3 s to the w

BEFORE AND AFTER

CLUE

door ______ sign

Answer:
*door **stop** sign*

Before and After #1

Find the word that follows the first word and precedes the second word.

CLUE

door _____ sign

Answer:
*door **stop** sign*

1. water _________ house

2. head _________ bulb

3. pass _________ drive

4. book _________ room

5. hand _________ rack

6. wall _________ bag

7. under _________ over

8. bottle _________ lace

Before and After #2

Find the word that follows the first word and precedes the second word.

CLUE

door _____ sign

Answer:
*door **stop** sign*

1.

dog ________ key

2.

sign ________ office

3.

fountain ________ pal

4.

pop ________ flakes

5.

apple ________ plate

6.

special ________ boy

7.

shoe ________ office

8.

up ________ down

Before and After #3

Find the word that follows the first word and precedes the second word.

CLUE

door _____ sign

Answer:
door ***stop*** *sign*

1.

bird ________ boat

2.

stop ________ house

3.

net ________ out

4.

over ________ rack

5.

ceiling ________ fare

6.

car ________ room

7.

bubble ________ wrapper

8.

car ________ man

Before and After #4

Find the word that follows the first word and precedes the second word.

CLUE

door _____ sign

Answer:
*door **stop** sign*

1.

board _________ way

2.

master _________ meal

3.

caution _________ house

4.

baby _________ house

5.

shoe _________ case

6.

rubber _______ collection

7.

front _________ frame

8.

paradise _________ soul

Before and After #5

Find the word that follows the first word and precedes the second word.

CLUE

door _____ sign

Answer:
*door **stop** sign*

1.

table _________ dog

2.

shoe ________ tablecloth

3.

flat _________ iron

4.

dollar _________ board

5.

gas _________ top

6.

stone _________ board

7.

dish _________ fluid

8.

theater _________ stub

Before and After #6

Find the word that follows the first word and precedes the second word.

CLUE

door _____ sign

Answer:
door ***stop*** *sign*

1.

gas _________ iron

2.

ceiling _________ mail

3.

apple _________ values

4.

ski _________ camp

5.

skim _________ shake

6.

car _________ bell

7.

bowling _________ grass

8.

sugar _________ furniture

Before and After #7

Find the word that follows the first word and precedes the second word.

CLUE

door _____ sign

Answer:
*door **stop** sign*

1.

ski _________ top

2.

bowling ________ point

3.

computer _________ trap

4.

coffee _________ tip

5.

swivel _________ man

6.

side _________ map

7.

target _________ star

8.

dead _________ run

Before and After #8

Find the word that follows the first word and precedes the second word.

CLUE

door _____ sign

Answer:
door ***stop*** *sign*

1.

gravel _________ stop

2.

musical _________ paper

3.

better _________ mast

4.

egg _________ full

5.

peanut _________ cup

6.

front _________ way

7.

life _________ dancing

8.

paved _________ side

Before and After #9

Find the word that follows the first word and precedes the second word.

CLUE

door _____ sign

Answer:
*door **stop** sign*

1.

bottle _________ gun

2.

bus _________ sign

3.

skipping _________ ladder

4.

fast _________ chain

5.

police _________ port

6.

bare _________ stool

7.

hair _________ fire

8.

shoe _________ bag

Before and After #10

Find the word that follows the first word and precedes the second word.

CLUE

door _____ sign

Answer:
*door **stop** sign*

1.

bare _________ wax

2.

hair _________ off

3.

big _________ machine

4.

bald _________ light

5.

sold _________ side

6.

tall _________ wreck

7.

last _________ girl

8.

corn _________ shirt

Before and After #11

Find the word that follows the first word and precedes the second word.

CLUE

door _____ sign

Answer:
*door **stop** sign*

1.

guess _________ ever

2.

dog _________ keeper

3.

best _________ ship

4.

plastic _________ general

5.

store _________ boat

6.

cruise _________ shape

7.

pop _________ husk

8.

make _________ work

Before and After #12

Find the word that follows the first word and precedes the second word.

CLUE

door _____ sign

Answer:
*door **stop** sign*

1.

dart _________ game

2.

paper _________ lifting

3.

cattle _________ dance

4.

checker _________ walk

5.

corn _________ goal

6.

rock _________ path

7.

kitchen _________ pipe

8.

pot _________ weight

Before and After #13

Find the word that follows the first word and precedes the second word.

CLUE

door _____ sign

Answer:
*door **stop** sign*

1.

fire _________ mat

2.

place _________ table

3.

summer _________ fire

4.

fruit _________ bar

5.

trench _________ collar

6.

crow _________ stool

7.

fast _________ suit

8.

path _________ side

Before and After #14

Find the word that follows the first word and precedes the second word.

CLUE

door _____ sign

Answer:
*door **stop** sign*

1.

water _________ page

2.

cover _________ book

3.

head _________ up

4.

carry _________ going

5.

dump _________ load

6.

shoe _________ rimmed

7.

play _________ hockey

8.

blue _________ light

MISSING LETTER

Missing Letter #1

Each of the following spells a word. Find the missing letter.

CLUE

H S T E N G T

Answer:
STRENGTH
The Missing Letter is: R

1. R M F

2. A L M A N

3. S I T A L H O

4. E S P O N

5. I N T

Missing Letter #2

CLUE

S T E N G T H

Answer:
STRENGTH
The Missing Letter is: R

Each of the following spells a word. Find the missing letter.

1.

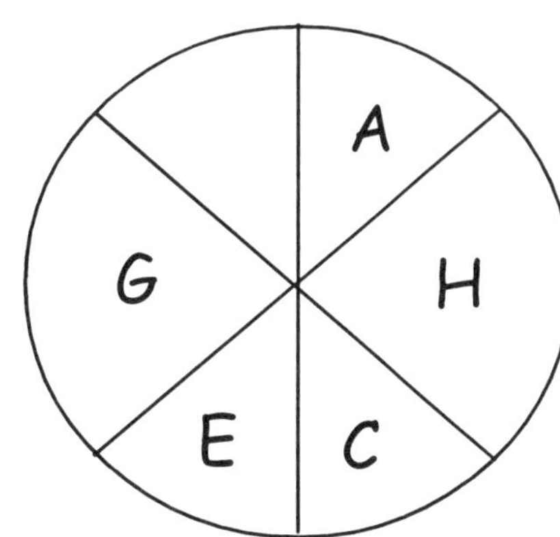

2.

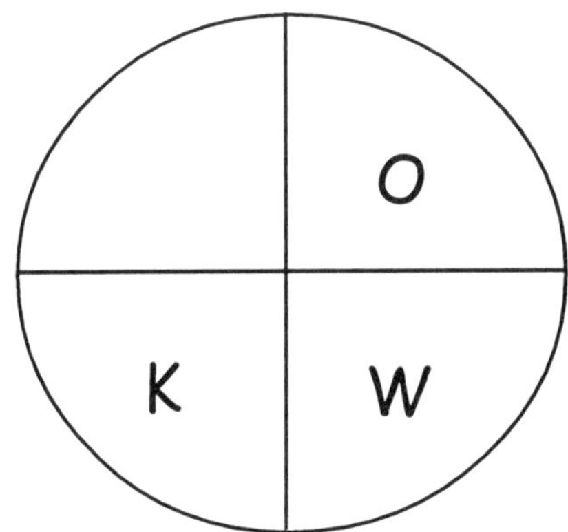

3.

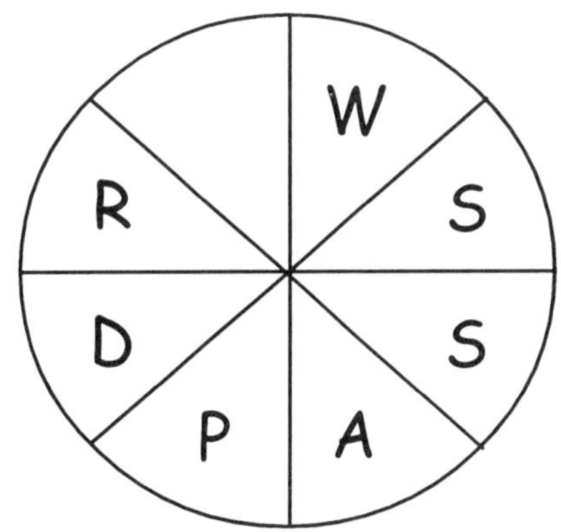

4.

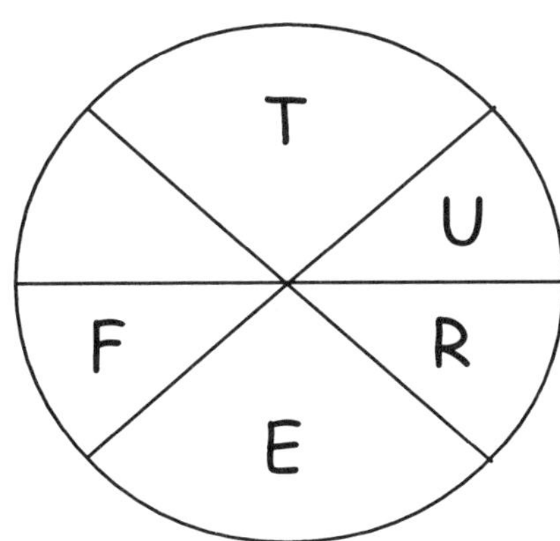

5.

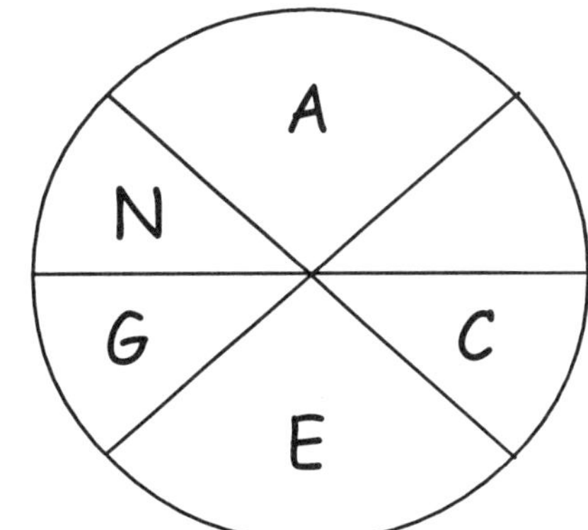

Missing Letter #3

CLUE

S T H T E G N

Answer:

STRENGTH

The Missing Letter is: R

Each of the following spells a word. Find the missing letter.

1\.

N T S P I

2\.

N I J

3\.

E D I N E B T

4\.

I L S P E

5\.

E R U M E P

Missing Letter #4

Each of the following spells a word. Find the missing letter.

CLUE

S T E N G T H (in circle)

Answer:
STRENGTH
The Missing Letter is: **R**

1.

P, (blank), E, E, N

2.

N, I, R, (blank)

3.

I, L, Y, G, R, (blank), E, D

4.

U, (blank), G, E, L, O

5.

(blank), U, D, E, P, R, E

Missing Letter #5

Each of the following spells a word. Find the missing letter.

CLUE

S T H T E G N

Answer:
STRENGTH
The Missing Letter is: **R**

1.

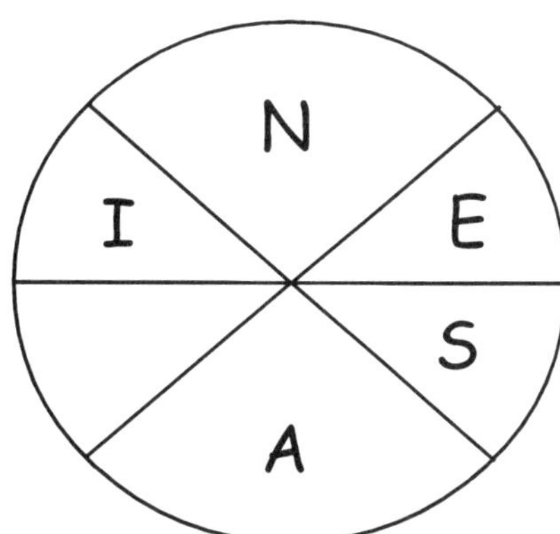

2.

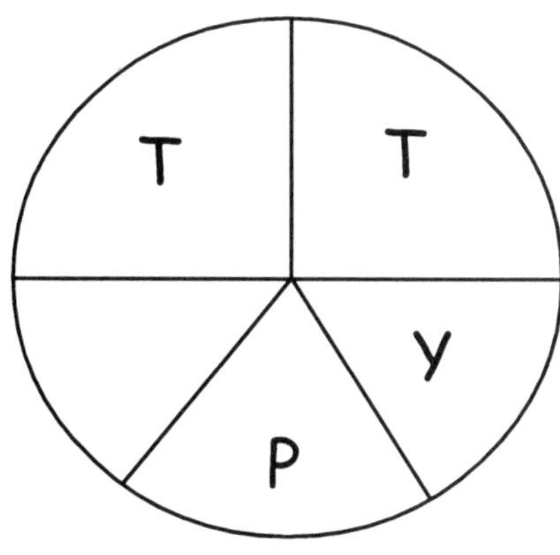

3.

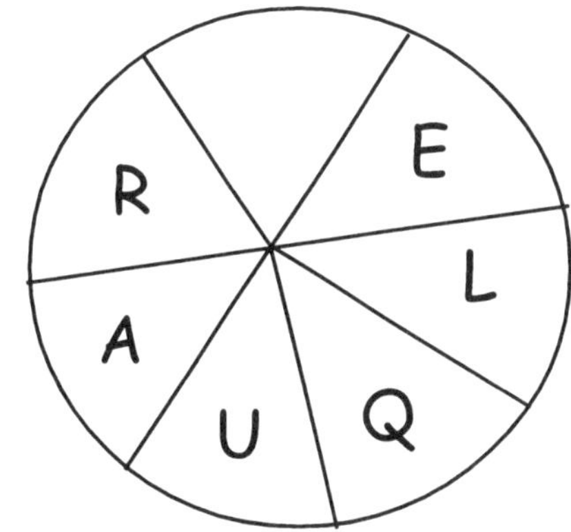

4.

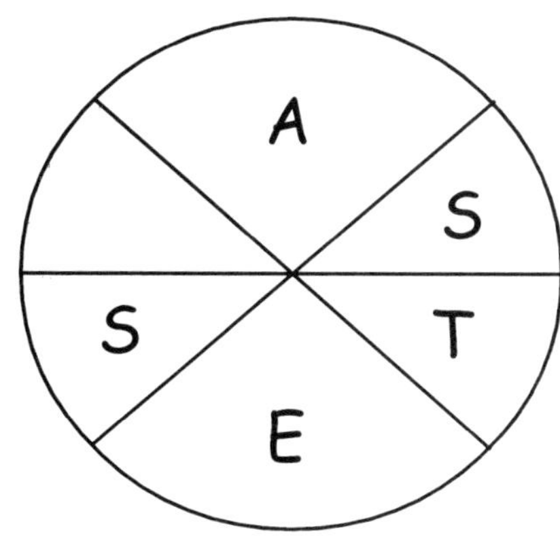

5.

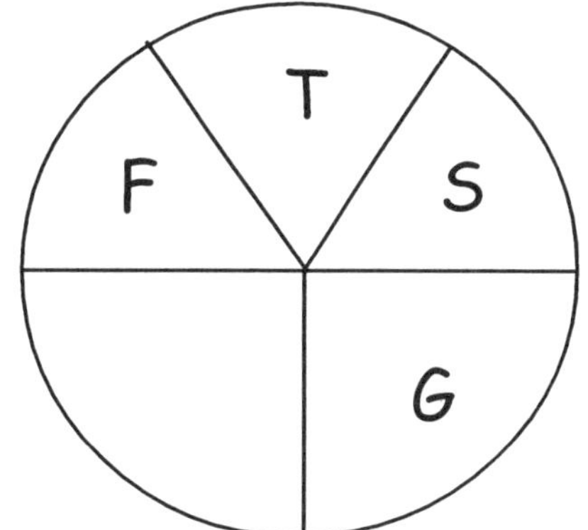

Missing Letter #6

CLUE

S T E N G T H

Answer:
STRENGTH
The Missing Letter is: **R**

Each of the following spells a word. Find the missing letter.

1.

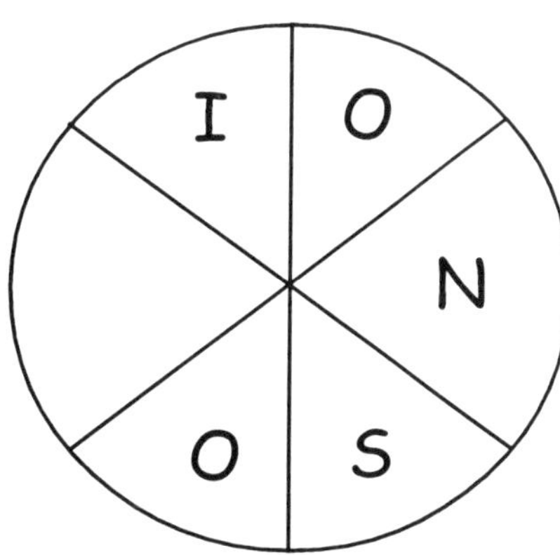

2.

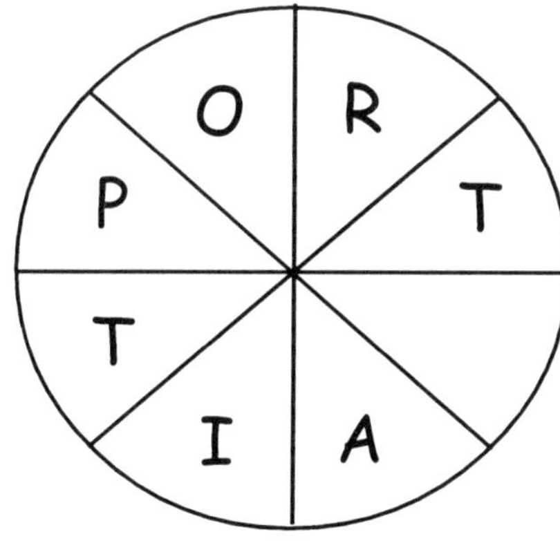

3.

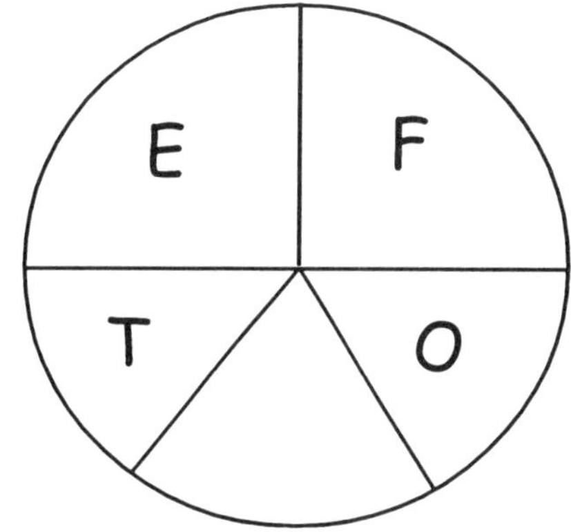

4.

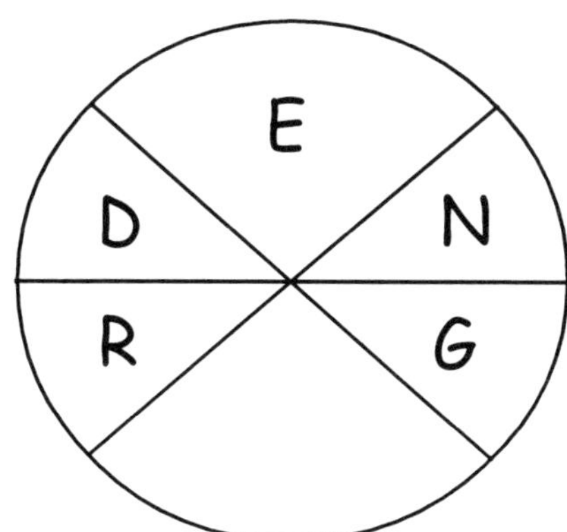

5.

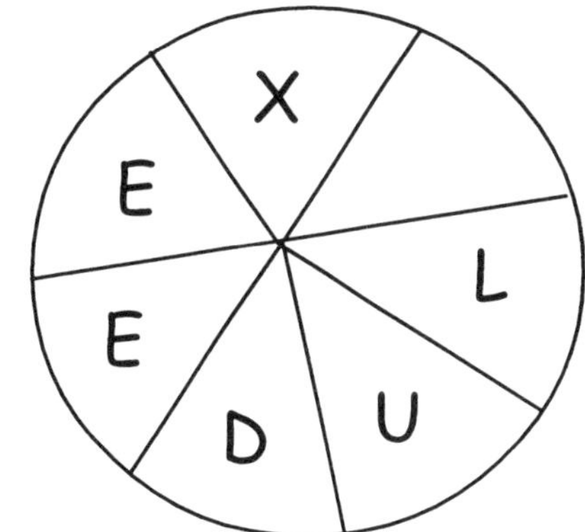

Missing Letter #7

CLUE

S T H T E G N

Answer:
STRENGTH
The Missing Letter is: **R**

Each of the following spells a word. Find the missing letter.

1.

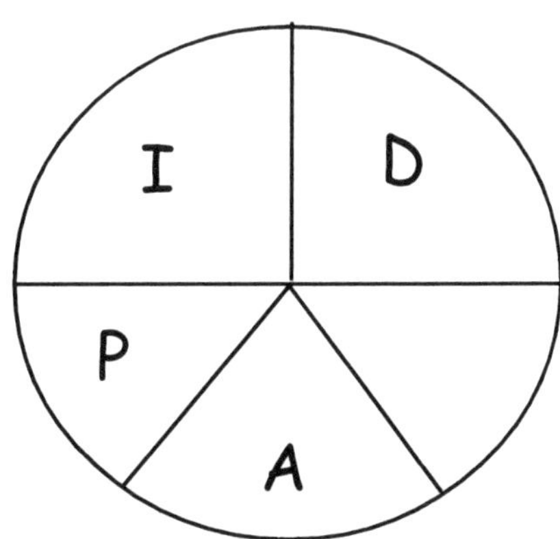

2.

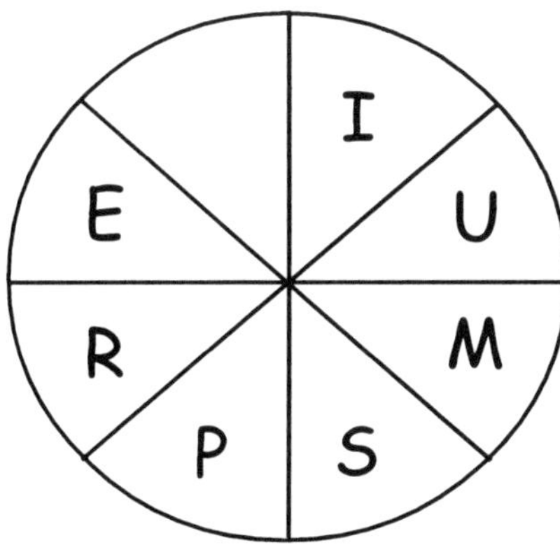

3.

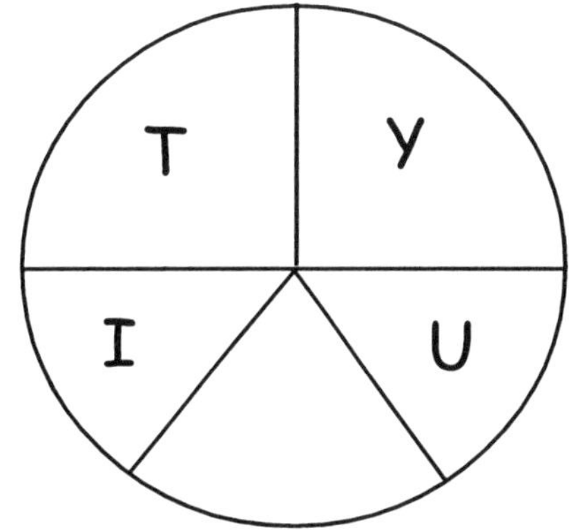

4.

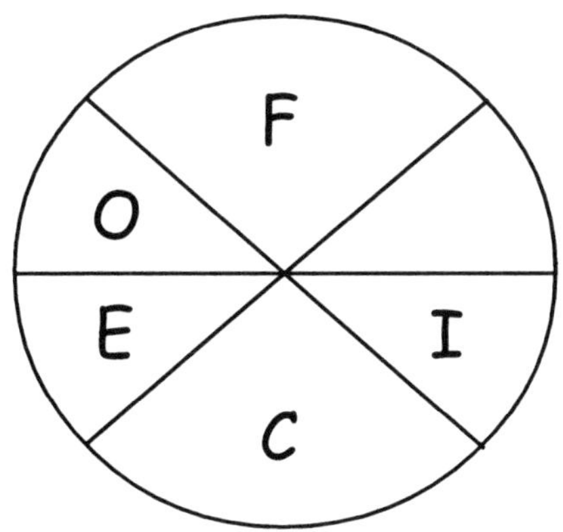

5.

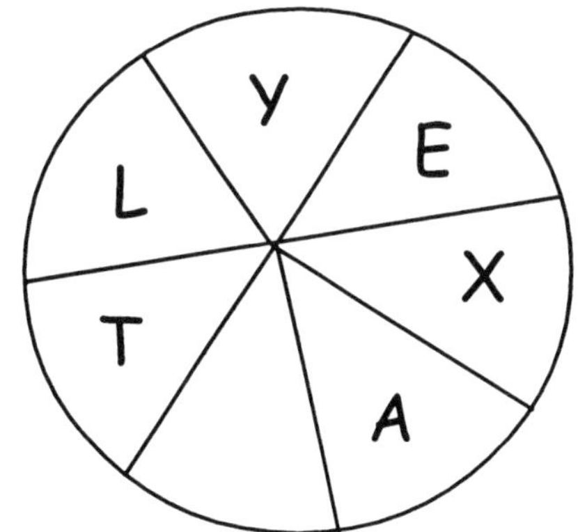

Missing Letter #8

Each of the following spells a word. Find the missing letter.

CLUE

S, T, E, N, G, T, H

Answer:

STRENGTH

The Missing Letter is: R

1.

I, N, C, T, I, N, S

2.

E, O, C, R

3.

T, I, U, C, S, B

4.

H, T, R, O, U, G

5.

O, N, B

PICTURE IT

Picture It #1

CLUE

Answer:
Fast Food

Find the expression or phrase that each of these represents.

1.

2.

3.

4.

5.

6.

Picture It #2

Find the expression or phrase that each of these represents.

CLUE

Answer:
Fast Food

1.

2.

3.

4.

5.

6.

it

Picture It #3

Find the expression or phrase that each of these represents.

In a Timely Manner

CLUE

Answer:
Fast Food

1.

Pay 4 

2.

3.

4.

5.

6.

HOC  KEY

MIXED BAG

CLUE

blflowersoom

Answer:
flowers in bloom

CLUE

scar
lag
rile

Answer: ***f***
scarf
flag
rifle

CLUE

Napkin
Nose
Circus

Answer:
ring

CLUE

door ______ sign

Answer:
door ***stop*** *sign*

CLUE

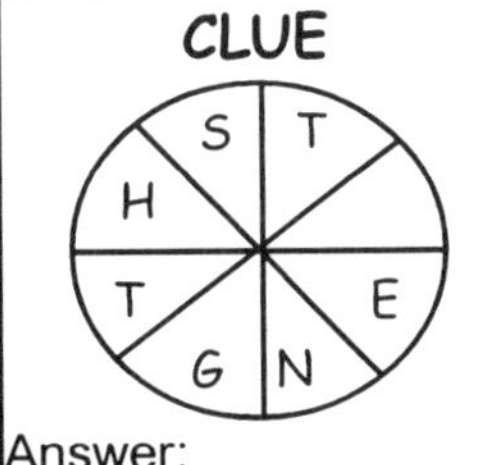

Answer:
STRENGTH
The Missing Letter is: R

CLUE

12	(33)	55
14	( )	25

Answer: ***11***
The difference between the numbers outside the brackets

Mixed Bag #1

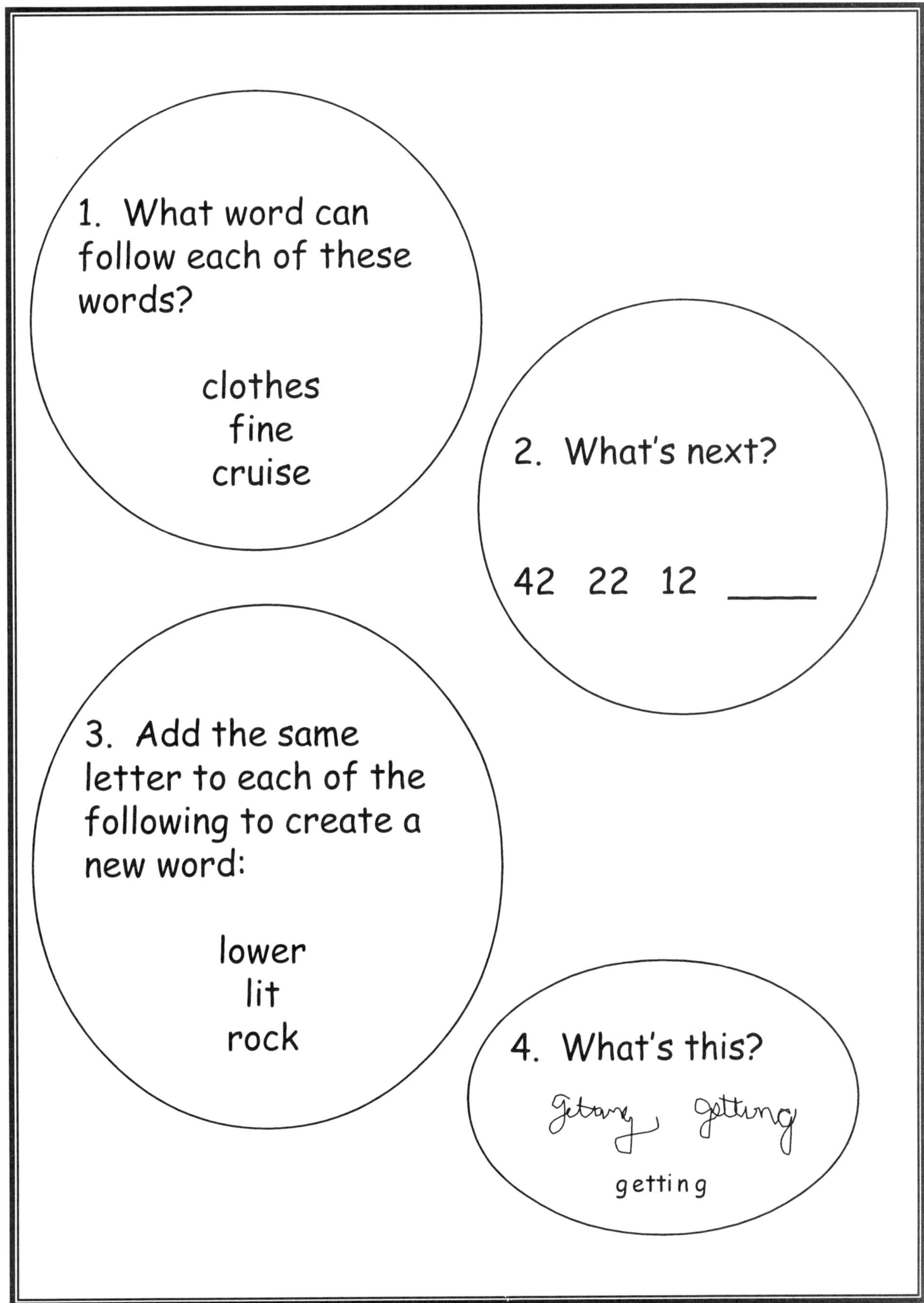
1. What word can follow each of these words?
clothes
fine
cruise
2. What's next?
42 22 12 ____
3. Add the same letter to each of the following to create a new word:
lower
lit
rock
4. What's this?
getting

Mixed Bag #2

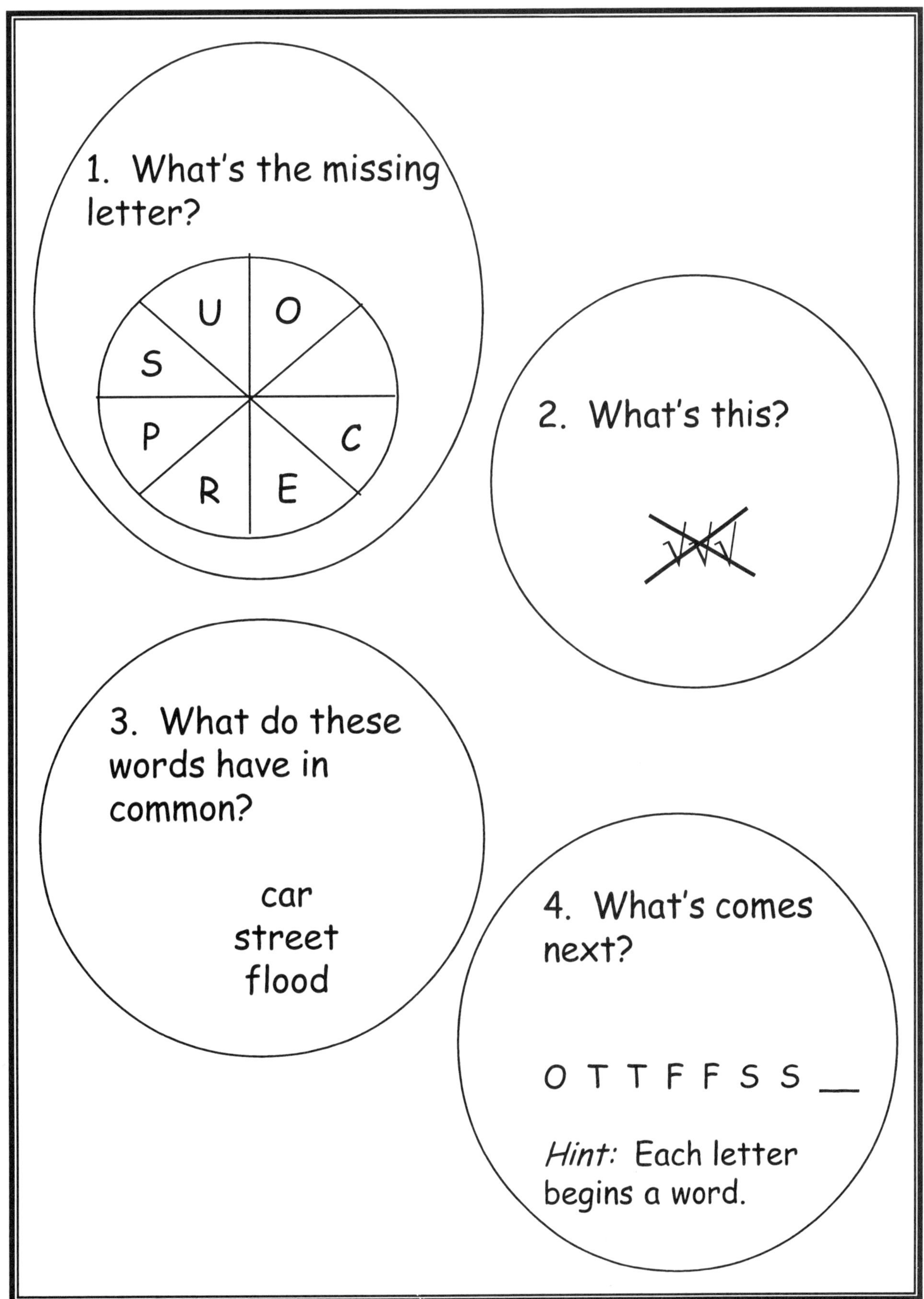
1. What's the missing letter?
U
O
S
C
P
E
R
2. What's this?
3. What do these words have in common?
car
street
flood
4. What's comes next?
O T T F F S S __
Hint: Each letter begins a word.

Mixed Bag #3

1. What's missing?

196 (25) 324
329 (   ) 137

2. Add the same letter to each of the following to create a new word:

tire
rip
roll

3. What's this?

basicsgnitteg

4. What's the missing letter?

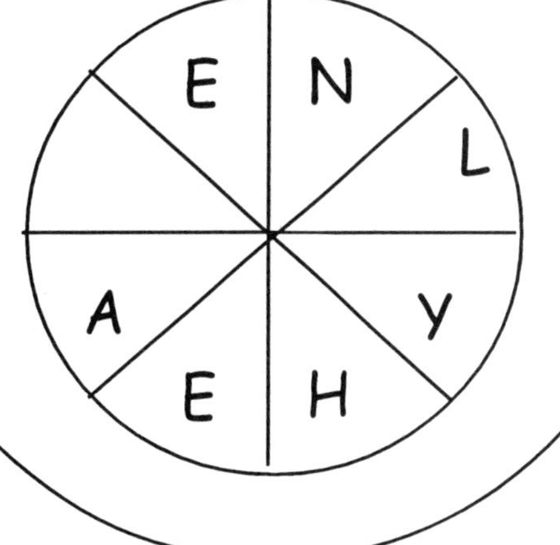

Mixed Bag #4

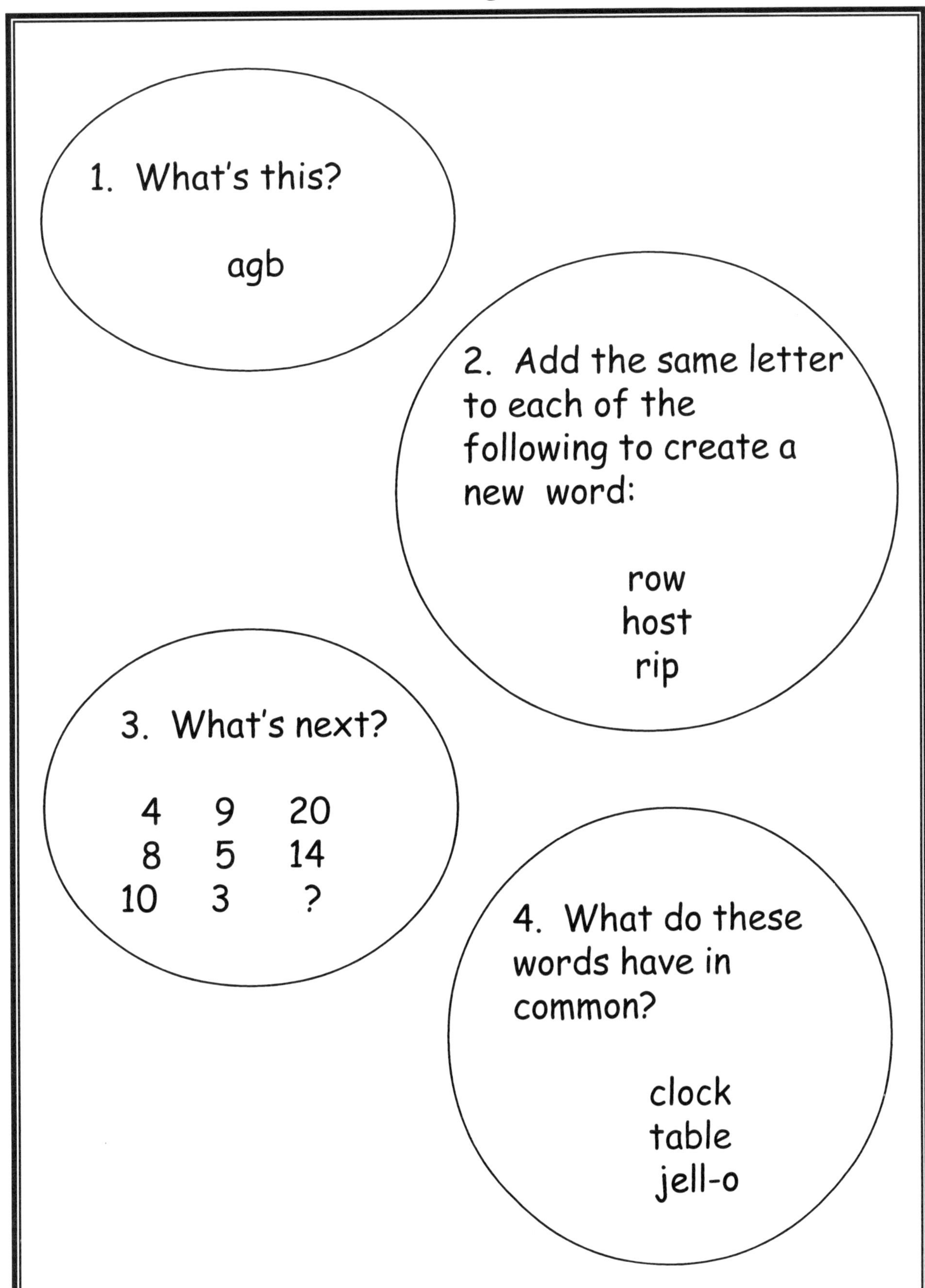
1. What's this?
agb
2. Add the same letter to each of the following to create a new word:
row
host
rip
3. What's next?
4 9 20
8 5 14
10 3 ?
4. What do these words have in common?
clock
table
jell-o

Mixed Bag #5

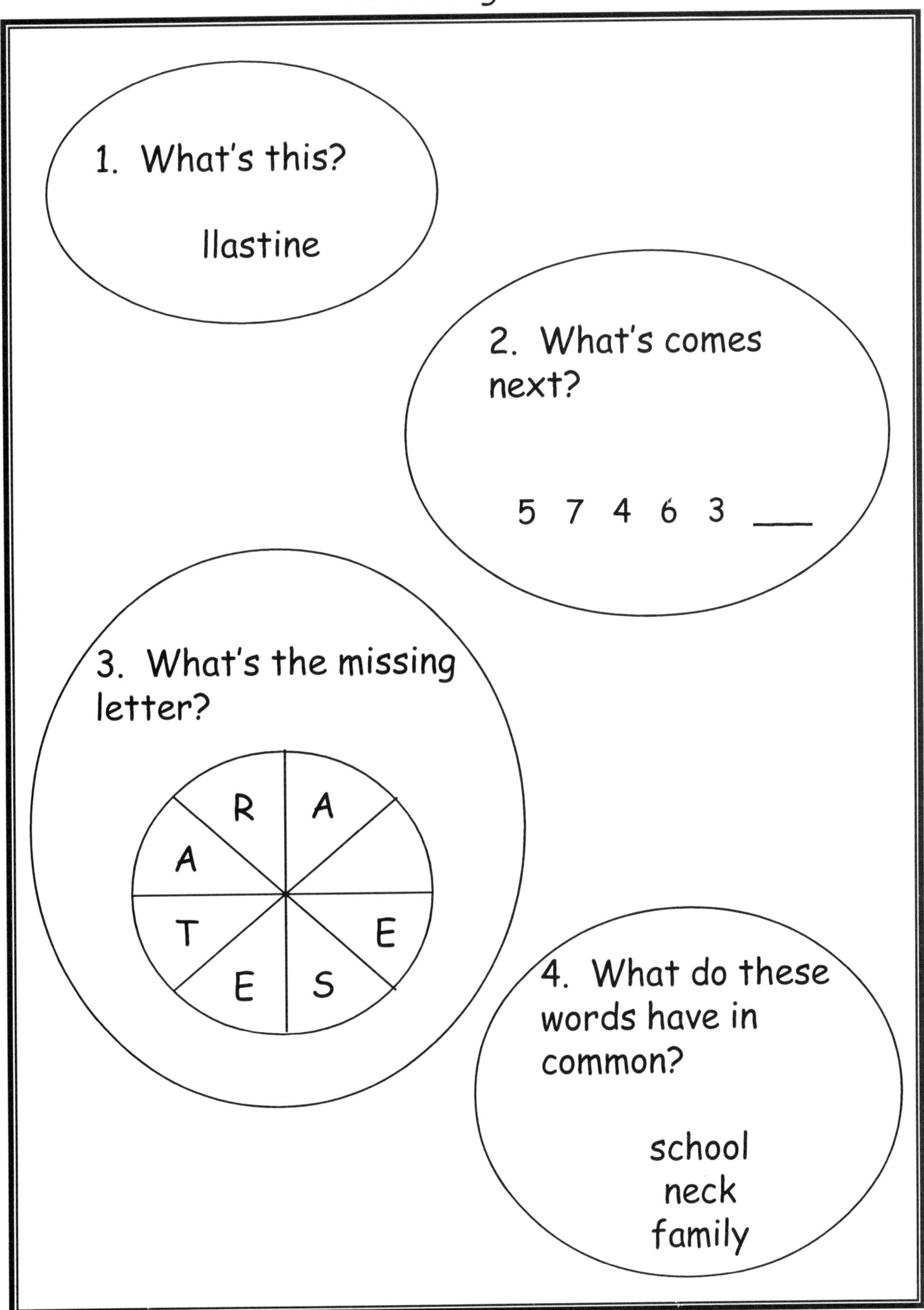
1. What's this?
llastine
2. What's comes next?
5 7 4 6 3 ___
3. What's the missing letter?
R
A
E
S
E
T
A
4. What do these words have in common?
school
neck
family

Mixed Bag #6

1. What's the missing letter?

2. What do these words have in common?

fly
wall
writing

3. What's this?

over over
over over
over over
over over
over over

4. Insert the missing number?

16 (27) 43
29 ( ) 56

Mixed Bag #7

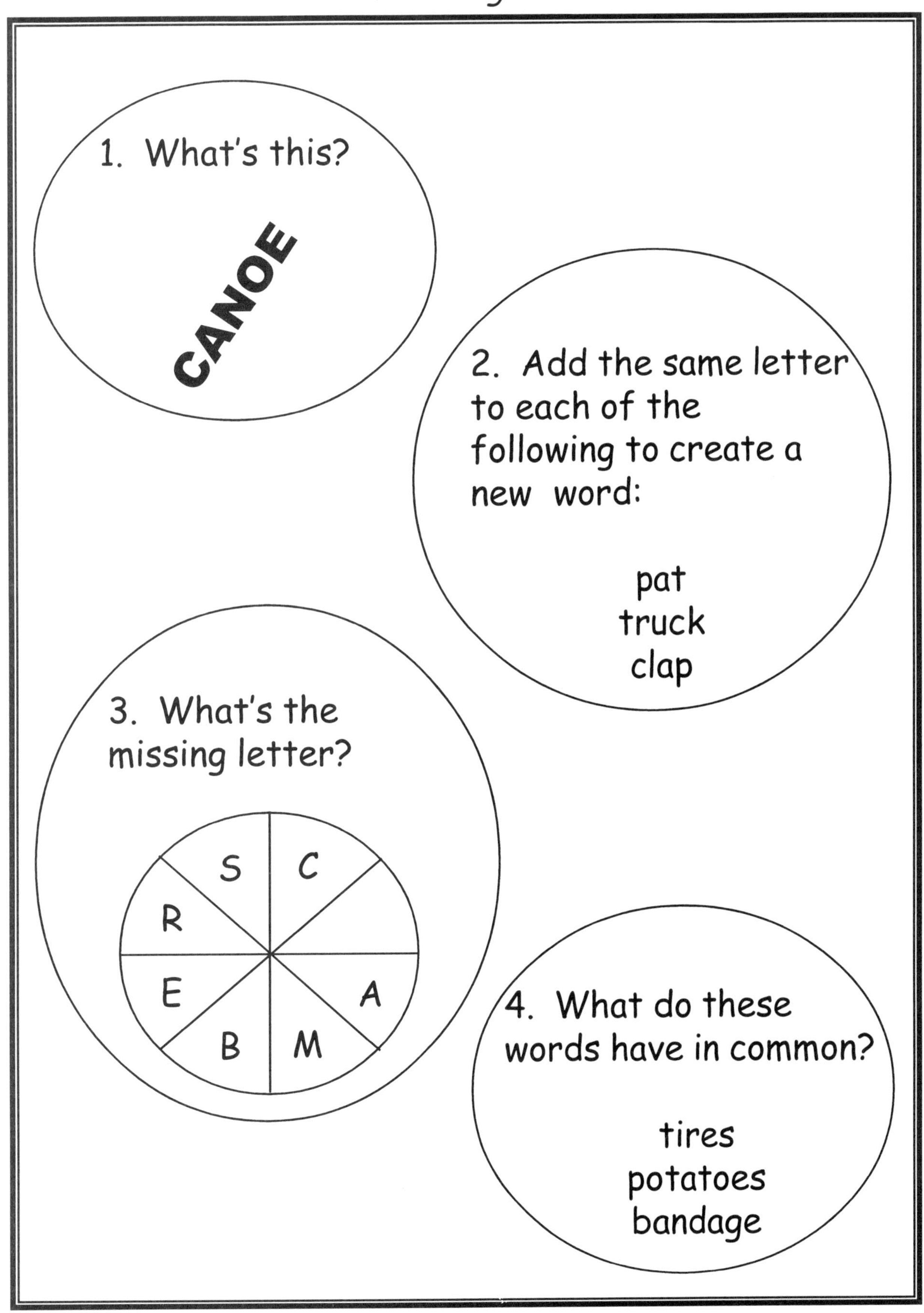
1. What's this?
CANOE
2. Add the same letter to each of the following to create a new word:
pat
truck
clap
3. What's the missing letter?
S
C
R
E
A
B
M
4. What do these words have in common?
tires
potatoes
bandage

Mixed Bag #8

1. What's this?

littlelittle

2. What do these words have in common:

elevator
face
weight

3. Add the same letter to each of the following to create a new word:

gasp
evolve
each

4. Insert the missing number?

16	(93)	15
14	( )	12

Mixed Bag #9

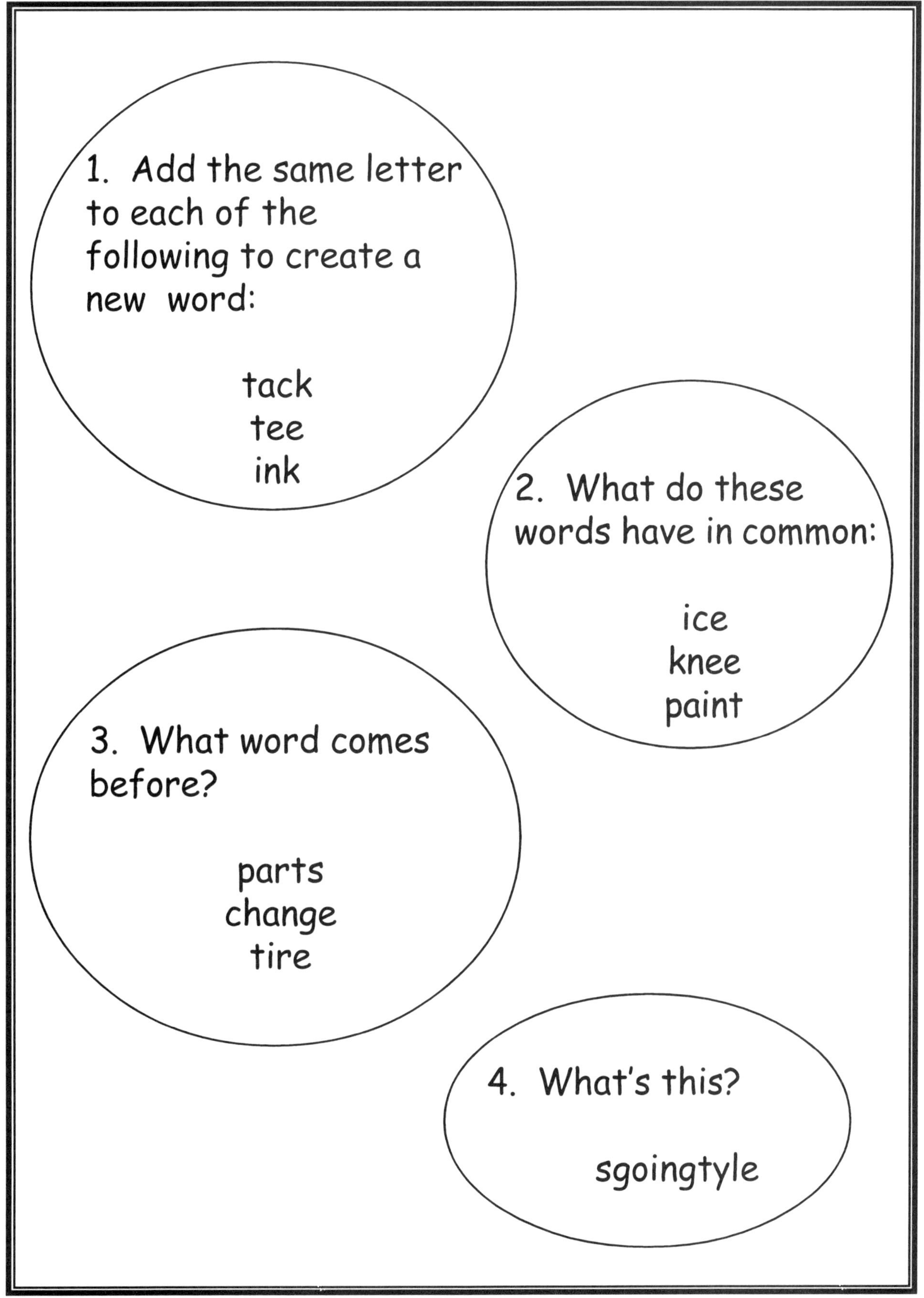
1. Add the same letter to each of the following to create a new word:
tack
tee
ink
2. What do these words have in common:
ice
knee
paint
3. What word comes before?
parts
change
tire
4. What's this?
sgoingtyle

Mixed Bag #10

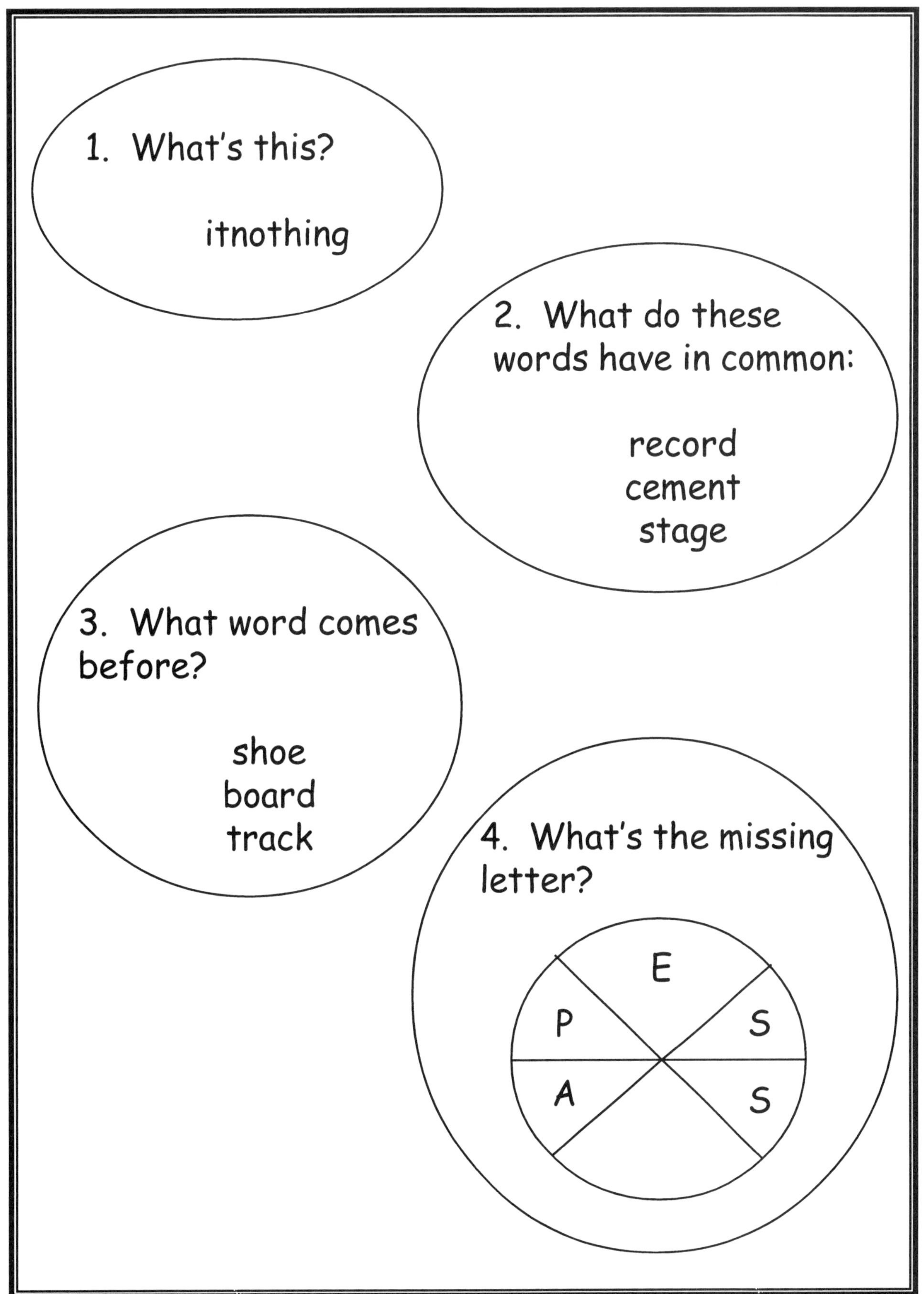

1. What's this?
itnothing
2. What do these words have in common:
record
cement
stage
3. What word comes before?
shoe
board
track
4. What's the missing letter?
E
S
S
A
P

Mixed Bag #11

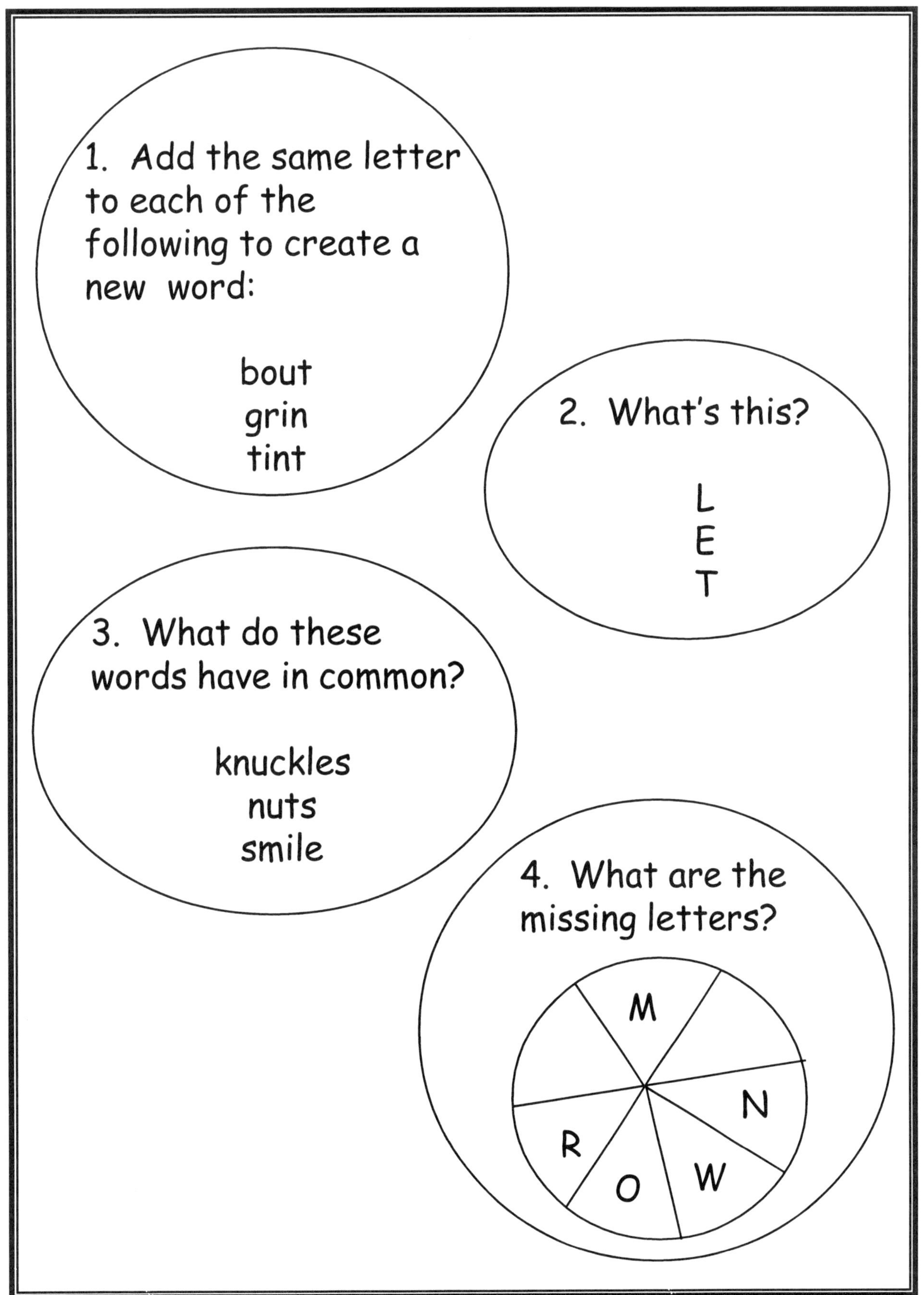
1. Add the same letter to each of the following to create a new word:
bout
grin
tint
2. What's this?
L
E
T
3. What do these words have in common?
knuckles
nuts
smile
4. What are the missing letters?
M
N
W
O
R

Mixed Bag #12

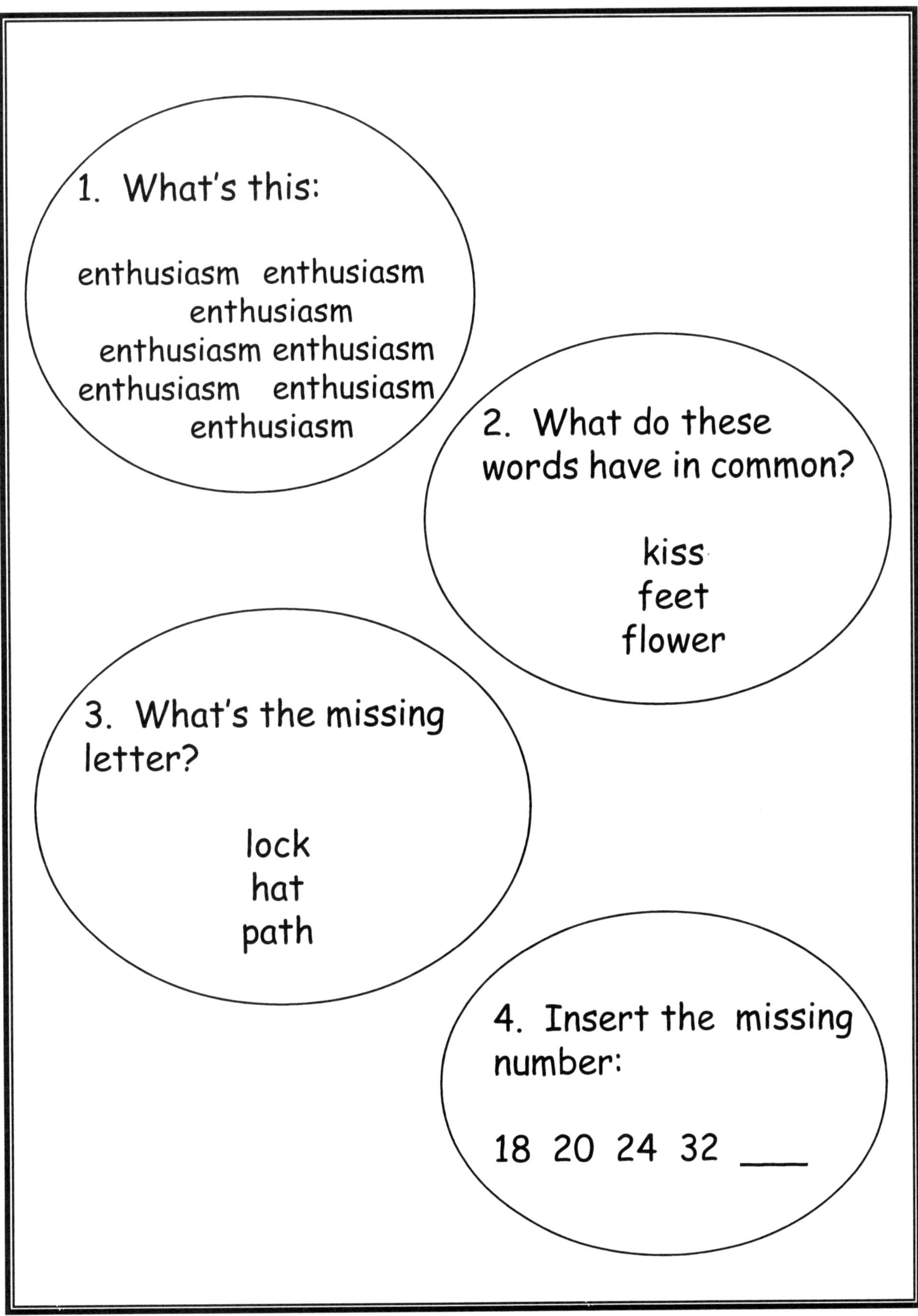
1. What's this:
enthusiasm enthusiasm
enthusiasm
enthusiasm enthusiasm
enthusiasm enthusiasm
enthusiasm
2. What do these words have in common?
kiss
feet
flower
3. What's the missing letter?
lock
hat
path
4. Insert the missing number:
18 20 24 32 ___

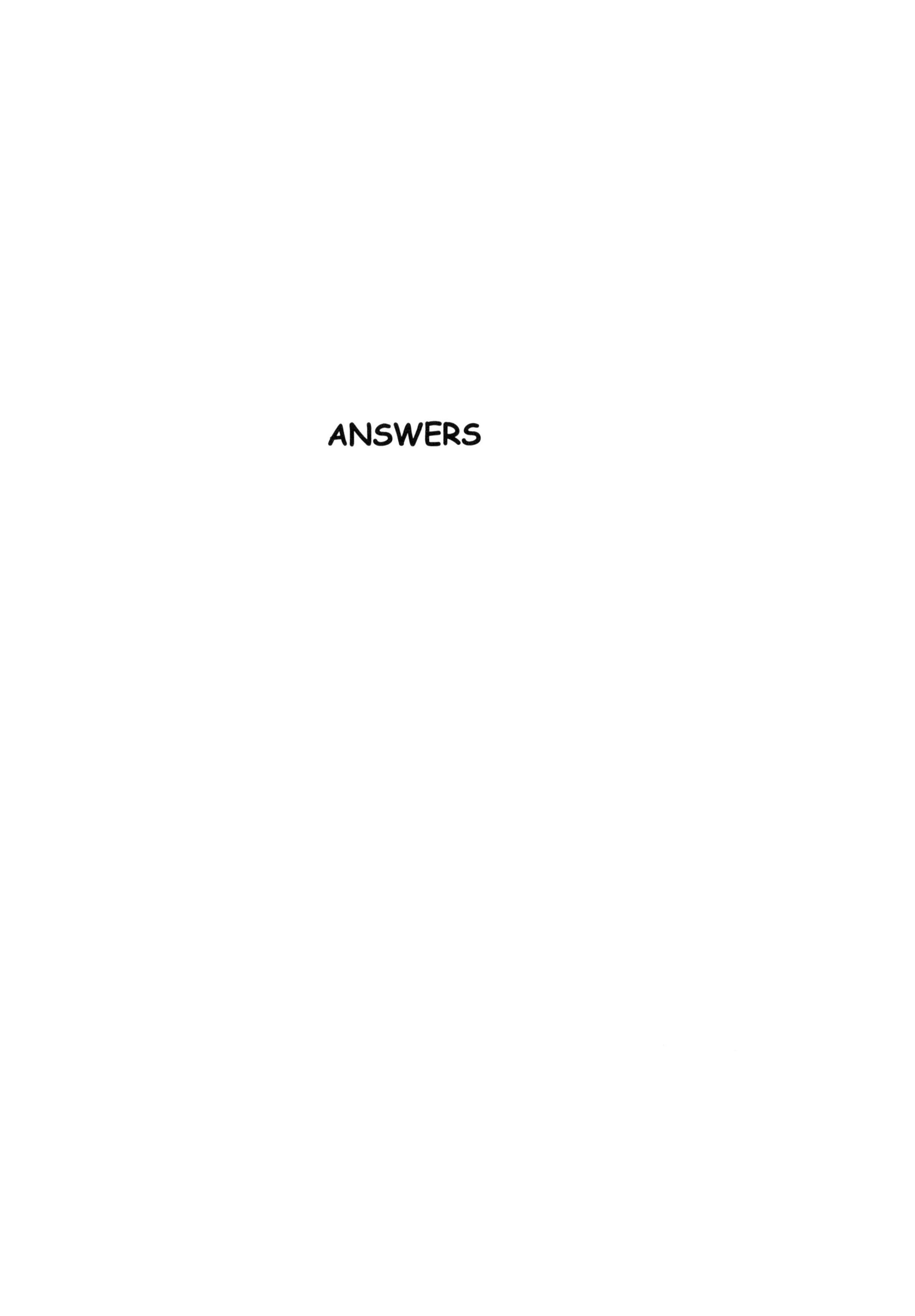

ANSWERS

Answers
Brain Teasers

Brain Teaser #1
Page 3

1. Flat tire
2. 3 degrees above zero
3. Short lived
4. Fine line
5. Paratrooper
6. Puff pastry
7. 2-faced or about face
8. Around the corner

Brain Teaser #2
Page 5

1. Lighten up
2. Being at the end of your rope
3. Quick turnaround
4. Buzz me up
5. Bottom line
6. The eye of the hurricane
7. Splitting hairs
8. Catcher in the rye

Brain Teaser #3
Page 7

1. Noah's Ark
2. Turned up nose
3. Bottom rung
4. An after thought
5. Straight up
6. Come in under budget
7. Wrong turn
8. Twisted mind

Brain Teaser #4
Page 9

1. High jinx
2. He's down in the dumps
3. You're up to the limit
4. Broadway
5. Straight jacket
6. Start at the beginning of the story
7. Turn against him
8. Get off at the end of the line

Brain Teaser #5
Page 11

1. Curved space
2. Three way tie
3. Repeat yourself
4. An upstart or start up
5. Looking beyond the obvious
6. Matching pair
7. He got it backwards
8. Barometer rising

Brain Teaser #6
Page 13

1. Going overboard
2. Periscope
3. Persian Gulf
4. Hard work
5. A piece of my mind
6. Forewarning
7. I'm better than ever
8. Short circuit

Brain Teaser #7
Page 15

1. People in high places
2. Expressway
3. Break the bank
4. Basic instinct
5. Hands down
6. Living alone
7. Heavy handed
8. Pre-meditated murder

Brain Teaser #8
Page 17

1. Uphill battle
2. She's on top of the world
3. Missing link
4. Travelling back and forth
5. Undercover agent
6. Throw up
7. He's in the red
8. The joke is on you

Brain Teaser #9
Page 19

1. Bet on a dark horse
2. Diamond in the rough
3. Corner the market
4. Penniless
5. Double exposure
6. Missing you in summer
7. Miniature golf
8. Short story

Brain Teaser #10
Page 21

1. Growing pains
2. Breaking news
3. High jump
4. Climbing ivy
5. Twice blessed
6. Low return on investment
7. Drive-in theatre
8. Sand pile

Brain Teaser #11
Page 23

1. No second chance
2. He's deeply in debt
3. Layer cake
4. Changing times
5. Once upon a time
6. Getting it backwards
7. Full figure
8. Better safe than sorry

Brain Teaser #12
Page 25

1. It's beyond me
2. Working overtime
3. Paraphrase
4. Vicious circle
5. Top notch
6. Try again
7. Skip breakfast
8. Castles in the air

Brain Teaser #13
Page 27

1. Break the tie
2. Start over again
3. Murder investigation
4. Smokestack
5. Growing concern
6. Practice makes perfect
7. Button-down collar
8. All above board

Brain Teaser #14
Page 29

1. Lots of money
2. Running down hill
3. Online trading
4. Paramount importance
5. Wedding ring
6. Sing in harmony
7. Close up
8. Disappearing act

Brain Teaser #15
Page 31

1. High stakes
2. Shrinking violet
3. Strong under pressure
4. It is in the top drawer
5. Chess mate
6. Slipped up
7. Dominoes
8. Second hand clothes

Brain Teaser #16
Page 33

1. Repeated question
2. Small stuff
3. Underwater exploration
4. Growing deficit
5. Sitting duck
6. Fascination
7. Cross-eyed
8. Politically correct

Brain Teaser # 17
Page 35

1. Cabin in the woods
2. Well brought up
3. Hole in one
4 Last nail in the coffin
5. Drug addict
6. Sixth sense
7. Pair of shoes
8. He over spent and under earned

Brain Teaser #18
Page 37

1. Wheel spinning
2. Big top
3. Fill in the blank
4. Paramedic
5. Copy cat
6. Repeat performance
7. Time after time
8. Scattered thoughts

Brain Teaser #19
Page 39

1. Tense moment
2. Divided highway
3. Revolving door
4. Solitary confinement
5. Just between friends
6. Growing evidence
7. Right hand turn
8. She's above reproach

Brain Teaser #20
Page 41

1. Silent majority
2. Reverse decision
3. She's bigger than life
4. Grand stand
5. Paranoid
6. Backfire
7. About face
8. Roll of thunder

Brain Teaser #21
Page 43

1. Close calls
2. Blackmail
3. Cut down
4. Clamp down on it
5. Mixed messages
6. It's on the tip of my tongue
7. Lone Ranger
8. He's up to no good

Brain Teaser #22
Page 45

1. He's down and out
2. He's after women
3. Go round in circles
4. Turn him over to the law
5. Give up
6. Tall ship
7. Parasail
8. Read between the lines

Brain Teaser #23
Page 47

1. Clowning around
2. Wave the penalty
3. It's beyond belief
4. He's between jobs
5. Back breaking work
6. Eggs over easy
7. I am falling in love
8. Fed up

Brain Teaser #24
Page 49

1. He is following the crowd
2. She stands out in a crowd
3. Switching places
4. Breaking rank
5. A piece of advice
6. A bunch of hooligans
7. He's above suspicion
8. Mountain climbing

Brain Teaser #25
Page 51

1. Landslide
2. It's up in the air
3. Come down to earth
4. A giant among men
5. Big deal
6. A piece of cake
7. Black eye
8. Reverse order

Brain Teaser #26
Page 53

1. Better late than never
2. Backpack
3. Breakdown
4. Without a leg to stand on
5. Jewel in the crown
6. Days on end
7. Divided loyalties
8. I'm broke

Brain Teaser #27
Page 55

1. A bunch of idiots
2. There's friction between them
3. Windfall
4. Fight over money
5. He's up to his knees in alligators
6. Without a care in the world
7. Making it big
8. Fingers in several pies

Brain Teaser #28
Page 57

1. Marked down
2. Pay back
3. No end in sight
4. Play it again
5. Half mast
6. Great escape
7. Loose leaf book
8. Overseas trip

Brain Teaser #29
Page 59

1. Different perspectives
2. Big wheel
3. Broken arrow
4. Make up
5. Chicken little
6. A bunch of roses
7. Light at the end of the tunnel
8. Slanted opinion

Brain Teaser #30
Page 61

1. Many mansions
2. Hill climbing
3. Friends in high places
4. Let's make up
5. Double your money
6. Being independent
7. Burning the candle at both ends
8. Head on collision

Brain Teaser #31
Page 63

1. Many points of view
2. Long weekend
3. It's in the bag
4. Wall to wall carpet
5. Think twice about it
6. Eyes bigger than stomach
7. Underground economy
8. Going up the wall

Brain Teaser #32
Page 65

1. Wake-up call
2. High school
3. He's underhanded
4. Building wealth
5. Car insurance
6. Flat broke
7. Double-decker bus
8. Ship in a bottle

Brain Teaser #33
Page 67

1. Down load
2. Short cut
3. A walk in the park
4. Knowledge gap
5. A gang of thugs
6. Turn coat
7. Jagged edge
8. Truth is stranger than fiction

Brain Teaser #34
Page 69

1. Big frog in a little puddle
2. Genie in a bottle
3. Double Dutch
4. Walk backwards
5. Bet on it
6. A bunch of flowers
7. Black hole
8. Global village

Brain Teaser #35
Page 71

1. Walking on thin ice
2. Last call
3. New innovation
4. Hair standing on end
5. Upper crust
6. Double vision
7. Too much over spending
8. Hitting close to home

Brain Teaser #36
Page 73

1. Paper thin
2. Last straw
3. All keyed up
4. Down turn in the economy
5. Double header
6. Performing past his peak
7. Starting out big
8. Clean from top to bottom

Brain Teaser #37
Page 75

1. Harmless fun
2. Indecent exposure
3. Curtain going up
4. Without a single regret
5. Hitting below the belt
6. Agree up to a point
7. New angle
8. Poor excuse

Brain Teaser #38
Page 77

1. Silk undergarment
2. Needle in a haystack
3. Forgone conclusion
4. Go over it again
5. Jumping to conclusions
6. Bridge mix
7. It's broken beyond repair
8. He's in a fog

Brain Teaser #39
Page 79

1. Try to understand
2. I'm unfulfilled without you
3. Turn the corner
4. Forewarned
5. Mixed emotions
6. Heavy metal
7. We are in the red
8. Sudden death overtime

Brain Teaser #40
Page 81

1. Joint account
2. Line up
3. Making ends meet
4. Rising inflation
5. She's falling to pieces
6. Misinformation
7. It's on again, off again
8. Going around the bush

Brain Teaser #41
Page 83

1. Partial agreement
2. Twin engine
3. Dark mood
4. Last in line
5. Blood is thicker than water
6. Sailing on the high seas
7. Live on the street
8. One after another

Brain Teaser #42
Page 85

1. Pirates on the high seas
2. Sundown
3. Turnaround
4. Breakfast in bed
5. Classified information
6. Slap in the face
7. Smuggling over the border
8. Big news

Brain Teaser #43
Page 87

1. Get to the end of the line
2. Forecast
3. Hole in the wall
4. Sundown
5. Broken heart
6. Banana split
7. Crying over spilled milk
8. The end is in sight

Brain Teaser #44
Page 89

1. Ante up
2. Poison pen letters
3. Erase the memory
4. Double take
5. A lesson in courage
6. Mixed vegetables
7. A cottage beside the sea
8. Best answer

Brain Teaser #45
Page 91

1. He's an underachiever
2. Long division
3. Last will and testament
4. Double indemnity
5. Group think
6. Parting of the ways
7. He's in the know
8. Backyard

Brain Teaser #46
Page 93

1. Undercover cop
2. Seven wonders of the world
3. Junk pile
4. Misinformation
5. Go down in flames
6. Play on words
7. A man among men
8. Mission statements

Brain Teaser #47
Page 95

1. Continuous improvement
2. Quality circles
3. Parachute
4. More or less
5. Turn on a dime
6. Viewpoint
7. Pig in a poke
8. Multi-millionaire

Brain Teaser #48
Page 97

1. Mark my words
2. Away (a way) in the manger
3. Are you up to it
4. Symphony without end
5. Dark secrets
6. She's spell bound
7. Run away from home
8. His days are numbered

Brain Teaser #49
Page 99

1. Its wrapped in secret
2. Broken egg
3. Fading memories
4. Mixed Blessings
5. Halfway house
6. One chance in a million
7. Foreign press
8. Getting over it

Brain Teaser #50
Page 101

1. Pie in the sky
2. Paranormal
3. Turn over a new leaf
4. Breakneck speed
5. Account overdrawn
6. You should be in pictures
7. He's between jobs
8. Inside information

Brain Teaser #51
Page 103

1. Sunset
2. Island in the sun
3. Feeling on top of the world
4. Back-up plan
5. Never ending story
6. Turning the world upside down
7. Dressed up
8. Pointed question

Brain Teaser #52
Page 105

1. Misunderstood
2. My heart in my mouth
3. Perfect pair
4. Down turn
5. Everything is upside down
6. Broken heart
7. Grateful
8. Altered states

Brain Teaser #53
Page 107

1. 2 peas in a pod
2. Lost in space
3. Advance on green
4. Instant replay
5. It is up to you
6. Reverse osmosis
7. m & n's
8. Skinny dip

Brain Teaser #54
Page 109

1. Deeply in debt
2. Cool under fire
3. The final judgment
4. Pointing a finger
5. Going at it alone
6. Double time
7. Flip side
8. Frazzled nerves

Brain Teaser #55
Page 111

1. Foreign exchange
2. Last resort
3. Twin engines
4. Flatulence
5. No way out
6. Icing on the cake
7. Fall down
8. Fender bender

Answers
What a Difference a Letter Makes

What a Difference a Letter Makes #1
Page 115

1. that
   tear
   trail
2. drum
   date
   dill
3. tray
   twig
   trip
4. bridge
   barb
   brace
5. rice
   rare
   taper
6. pride
   pace
   page
7. snake
   never
   kneel
8. grape
   rasp
   tree

What a Difference a Letter Makes #2
Page 117

1. grave
   ghost
   gape
2. caper
   brow
   tram
3. trade
   terror
   table
4. mind
   nail
   sand
5. liver
   grate
   brush
6. pray
   brow
   track
7. lease
   play
   lit
8. table
   bask
   bowl

What a Difference a Letter Makes #3
Page 19

1. shave
   hair
   shift
2. slate
   slow
   past
3. hair
   shear
   show
4. slice
   slip
   rasp
5. craft
   lice
   cramp
6. glass
   golden
   gamble
7. work
   wring
   rink
8. chair
   cup
   cable

What a Difference a Letter Makes #4
Page 121

1. able
   brush
   brim
2. gloat
   slide
   plaid
3. grave
   bread
   trickle
4. gravel
   saver
   track
5. crave
   related
   cover
6. trap
   rafter
   caper
7. fear
   fever
   fuse
8. glass
   gas
   glitter

What a Difference a Letter Makes #5
Page 123

1. around
   amaze
   glean
2. pear
   pram
   pace
3. drive
   carp
   raft
4. gown
   grind
   barge
5. chat
   hate
   chart
6. play
   ladder
   black
7. wall
   whip
   witch
8. trip
   trough
   twig

What a Difference a Letter Makes #6
Page 125

1. ship
   shave
   slick
2. frame
   brought
   grate
3. flood
   limp
   slave
4. sweat
   waft
   wax
5. rafter
   track
   grain
6. shake
   hat
   ship
7. gamble
   maim
   mass
8. plate
   slave
   lever

What a Difference a Letter Makes #7
Page 127

1. post
   slap
   ass
2. shoe
   soak
   spoke
3. bright
   black
   brag
4. break
   raft
   trick
5. tramp
   task
   trim
6. pant
   tramp
   tease
7. sliver
   slick
   supper
8. blame
   brave
   brim

What a Difference a Letter Makes #8
Page 129

1. peace
   pale
   cane
2. lice
   cramp
   clip
3. smile
   sword
   mast
4. rice
   brag
   frame
5. crush
   cash
   pact
6. skin
   sample
   slumber
7. able
   bear
   brow
8. hair
   champ
   hill

What a Difference a Letter Makes #9
Page 131

1. raft
   flower
   flock
2. prattle
   plump
   pram
3. cast
   spit
   clasp
4. heart
   grape
   race
5. brake
   caper
   bread
6. pact
   chair
   climb
7. glass
   grub
   gripe
8. able
   bill
   butter

What a Difference a Letter Makes #10
Page 133

1. burst
   brush
   related
2. tiger
   gold
   gas
3. table
   tale
   totter
4. plate
   pride
   plug
5. supper
   pass
   pout
6. putt
   trust
   tear
7. booth
   shake
   chat
8. spike
   spout
   ship

What a Difference a Letter Makes #11
Page 135

1. stone
   space
   star

2. four
   pound
   pout

3. thin
   hair
   thick

4. line
   nail
   many

5. master
   ramp
   time

6. mind
   known
   punt

7. blind
   lease
   play

8. said
   going
   paint

Answers
Something in Common

Something in Common #1
Page 139

1. You polish them
2. They each have a foot
3. They can be plugged
4. You can scratch them
5. The word post
6. You can spin them
7. The word climbing
8. The word board

Something in Common #2
Page 141

1. They are triangles
2. The word tablet
3. The word body
4. The word pour
5. They are types of pins
6. They are types of guides
7. The word grounds
8. They come in bars

Something in Common #3
Page 143

1. They can be sealed
2. Types of chips
3. Types of tickets
4. The word lock
5. You can load them
6. The word trailer
7. They can have a case
8. Coin can describe each

Something in Common #4
Page 145

1. The word net
2. They can be fast
3. The word line
4. Secret can describe each
5. They are types of paper
6. You skip them
7. They can be silent
8. The word call

Something in Common #5
Page 147

1. The word cone
2. You lead them
3. The word paper
4. They are types of crossings
5. They can be flat
6. They are types of cards
7. The word charge
8. They are types of bags

Something in Common #6
Page 149

1. The word short
2. The word roll
3. You read them
4. They are types of bags
5. They are types of frames
6. They can be set
7. You can open them
8. You post them

Something in Common #7
Page 151

1. The word stick
2. The word shred
3. The word shot
4. The word pop
5. The word pack
6. The word fork
7. They can be charged
8. The word hook

Something in Common #8
Page 153

1. The word switch
2. They are types of licenses
3. They are types of pens
4. You cut them
5. The word pick
6. They are types of stands
7. The word date
8. The word trunk

Something in Common #9
Page 155

1. The word purse
2. They each have a leaf
3. They each have a mouth
4. Short can describe each
5. The word erase
6. The word bow
7. They are types of caps
8. They are types of shells

Something in Common #10
Page 157

1. The word nose
2. They are types of bowls
3. Save them or spend them
4. Sharp can describe each
5. You run them
6. The word punch
7. The word shake
8. They have branches

Something in Common #11
Page 159

1. Things you run for
2. You paint them
3. They are types of brushes
4. You file them
5. The word pinch
6. The word pit
7. The word balance
8. You run them

Something in Common #12
Page 161

1. You launch them
2. Mother can describe each
3. You change them
4. Things you take
5. They all have shafts
6. The word poison
7. They can be tight
8. They all bend

Something in Common #13
Page 163

1. You change them
2. You can snap them
3. Things you seal
4. You stick them
5. You flip them
6. You cover them
7. You skip them
8. The word pack

Something in Common #14
Page 165

1. The word pack
2. The word pick
3. You mend them
4. You cut them
5. You play them
6. You build them
7. You raise them
8. You break them

Something in Common #15
Page 167

1. You can read them
2. You obey them
3. You collect them
4. Live up to them
5. You sit on them
6. You throw them
7. You open them
8. You can carve them

Something in Common #16
Page 169

1. You fix them
2. You pass them
3. Read them
4. You play on them
5. The word blow
6. You cut them
7. They can each describe the word force
8. You open them

Something in Common #17
Page 171

1. You close them
2. You shave them
3. You beat them
4. You repeat them
5. They are invisible
6. You fold them
7. You throw them
8. You take them

Something in Common #18
Page 173

1. You start them
2. You join them
3. They are types of openers
4. They are types of shows
5. The word top
6. The word gun
7. They can be bared
8. You tie them up

Something in Common #19
Page 175

1. The word path
2. The word key
3. The word stop
4. The word wire
5. They are types of signs
6. They are types of boots
7. The word paper
8. They all have strings

Something in Common #20
Page 177

1. They can be made of leather
2. They are types of bells
3. They are types of food
4. The word top
5. The word "push" precedes each
6. The word "powder" can follow each
7. The word "snow" precedes each
8. They are types of sticks

Something in Common #21
Page 179

1. The word "straw" precedes each
2. The word "cap" follows each
3. You can pull them
4. The word seed
5. You polish them
6. They each have a neck
7. You throw them
8. You can blow them

Something in Common #22
Page 181

1. You can break them
2. Water can describe each
3. The word pipe
4. They are types of books
5. Book can describe each
6. They have a center
7. Flag can describe each
8. The word "bell" precedes each

Something in Common #23
Page 183

1. They are types of crusts
2. The word hood
3. Strong can describe each
4. You skip them
5. The word pitch
6. You cut them
7. The word twist
8. The word sand can describe them

Something in Common #24
Page 185

1. You polish them
2. You snap them
3. You cross them
4. Rock can describe each
5. They are types of holes
6. You break them
7. You change them
8. You catch them

Something in Common #25
Page 187

1. The word pole
2. They are types of doors
3. You collect them
4. They can each describe the word cover
5. The word cover
6. You shampoo them
7. You change them
8. They are types of stools

Something in Common #26
Page 189

1. The word wax
2. They are types of cases
3. News can describe each
4. The can be set
5. Stop can describe each
6. The word sign
7. The word "prime" precedes each
8. They are types of poles

Something in Common #27
Page 191

1. The word trap
2. The word eye
3. They are types of shoes
4. The word "plate" follows each
5. The word post
6. The word cut
7. You break for them
8. They are types of boxes

Something in Common #28
Page 193

1. The word dog
2. They are types of jackets
3. Brass can describe each
4. The word paper
5. The word top
6. The word face
7. The word pool
8. The word "man" follows each

Answers
A Number of Things

A Number of Things #1
Page 197

1. 13 is a baker's dozen
2. 7 is a lucky number
3. 6 is a pack of beer
4. 45° in a right angle
5. 2 pints in a quart
6. 3 teaspoons in a tablespoon
7. 5 little pigs went to market
8. 12 inches in a foot

A Number of Things #2
Page 199

1. 3 blind mice
2. 10 dimes in a dollar
3. 76 trombones
4 12 months in a year
5. 29 days in Feb. in a leap year
6. 4 bases on a baseball diamond
7. 2 to tango
8. 7 wonders of the world

A Number of Things #3
Page 201

1. 7 dwarfs of Snow White
2. 3 Musketeers
3. 10 is Bo Derek's score
4. 26 letters in the alphabet
5. 52 cards in a deck
6. 2 shoes in a pair
7. 2 hands on a clock
8. 12 days of Christmas

A Number of Things #4
Page 203

1. 100 cents in a dollar
2. 7 deadly sins
3. 8 slices in a medium pizza
4. 12 disciples of Jesus
5. 5 cents in a nickel
6. 3 ring circus
7. 3 feet in a yard
8. 24 cokes in a case

A Number of Things #5
Page 205

1. 2 wheels on a bicycle
2. 2 peas in a pod
3. 4 prongs on a fork
4. 2 people in a pair of twins
5. 3 ringed binder
6. 4 quarters in a whole
7. 2 barrels in a shot gun
8. 4 leaf clover

A Number of Things #6
Page 207

1. 2 sides to a coin
2. 8 ounces in a half pound
3. 1 partridge in a pear tree
4. 4 lane highway
5. 40 days in the desert
6. 26 miles in a marathon
7. 4 suits in a deck of cards
8. 10 dimes in a dollar

A Number of Things #7
Page 209

1. 12 men in the dirty dozen
2. 9 innings in a baseball game
3. 12 members on a jury
4. 1 eyed Cyclops
5. 12 signs of the zodiac
6. 9 lives of a cat
7. 4 queens in a deck of cards
8. 3 sheets to the wind

Answers
Before and After

Before and After #1
Page 213

1. glass
2. light
3. over
4. store
5. towel
6. paper
7. pass
8. neck

Before and After #2
Page 215

1. house
2. post
3. pen
4. corn
5. pie
6. delivery
7. box
8. scale

Before and After #3
Page 217

1. house
2. light
3. work
4. coat
5. fan
6. wash
7. gum
8. door

Before and After #4
Page 219

1. walk
2. piece
3. light
4. doll
5. leather
6. stamp
7. door
8. lost

Before and After #5
Page 221

1. top
2. lace
3. tire
4. bill
5. tank
6. wall
7. washer
8. ticket

Before and After #6
Page 223

1. pump
2. fan
3. core
4. boot
5. milk
6. door
7. green
8. cane

Before and After #7
Page 225

1. hill
2. pin
3. mouse
4. filter
5. chair
6. road
7. shooting
8. end

Before and After #8
Page 227

1. pit
2. note
3. half
4. cup
5. butter
6. walk
7. line
8. road

Before and After #9
Page 229

1. cap
2. stop
3. rope
4. food
5. car
6. foot
7. brush
8. leather

Before and After #10
Page 231

1. floor
2. brush
3. time
4. head
5. out
6. ship
7. call
8. silk

Before and After #11
Page 233

1. what
2. house
3. friend
4. surgeon
5. house
6. ship
7. corn
8. shift

Page 235

1. board
2. weight
3. barn
4. board
5. field
6. garden
7. stove
8. light

Before and After #13
Page 237

1. place
2. card
3. camp
4. juice
5. coat
6. bar
7. track
8. way

Before and After #14
Page 239

1. front
2. story
3. line
4. on
5. truck
6. horn
7. ball
8. sky

Answers
Missing Letter

Missing Letter #1
Page 243

1. FORM
2. MANUAL
3. HOSPITAL
4. PHONES
5. INTO

Missing Letter #2
Page 245

1. CHARGE
2. WORK
3. PASSWORD
4. FUTURE
5. CHANGE

Missing Letter #3
Page 247

1. POINTS
2. JINX
3. INDEBTED
4. PERILS
5. PERFUME

Missing Letter #4
Page 249

1. PREEN
2. RINK
3. GREEDILY
4. LOUNGE
5. PRELUDE

Missing Letter #5
Page 251

1. SALINE
2. PUTTY
3. QUARREL
4. TASTES
5. GIFTS

Missing Letter #6
Page 253

1. ONIONS
2. PORTRAIT
3. FORTE
4. GARDEN
5. EXCLUDE

Missing Letter #7
Page 255

1. **R**APID
2. PRE**M**IUMS
3. U**N**ITY
4. OF**F**ICE
5. EXA**C**TLY

Missing Letter #8
Page 257

1. INS**T**INCT
2. CO**V**ER
3. B**I**SCUIT
4. **W**ROUGHT
5. BO**R**N

Answers
Picture It

Picture It #1
Page 261

1. Jumping to conclusions
2. Passing wind
3. Jam on the brakes
4. Turned back at the border
5. Paradise
6. Cut it short

Picture It #2
Page 263

1. Back to normal
2. Rest on Sundays
3. Picture perfect
4. Dead end
5. Thinking outside of the box
6. Banking on it

Picture It #3—In a Timely Manner
Page 265

1. Buying time
2. Time after time
3. Changing times
4. Running out of time
5. Time passes you by
6. Playing overtime in hockey

Answers
Mixed Bag

Mixed Bag #1
Page 269

1. line
2. **7**. Each number is obtained by adding 2 to the previous one, and then dividing by 2; 12 + 2 = 14; divided by 2 = 7.
3. flower
   lift
   frock
4. getting better

Mixed Bag #2
Page 271

1. precious
2. Cancelled checks
3. They are types of lights
4. **e**. eight. One, Two, Three, Four, Five, Six, Seven, Eight.

Mixed Bag #3
Page 273

1. **25**. Add the six digits outside the brackets together.
2. tired
   drip
   droll
3. getting back to basics
4. heavenly

Mixed Bag #4
Page 275

1. Mixed bag
2. grow
   ghost
   grip
3. **11**. Take half the first number in each horizontal row, add twice the second number, and you get the third.
4. You set them

Mixed Bag #5
Page 277

1. Last in line
2. 5. There are two different series of numbers: 5, 4, 3 and 7, 6, 5 (each in descending order).
3. Separate
4. They are types of ties

Mixed Bag #6
Page 279

1. Teamwork
2. They are types of paper
3. Leftovers
4. 27. The number in the brackets is the difference between the numbers outside the brackets.

Mixed Bag #7
Page 281

1. Tip the canoe
2. spat
   struck
   clasp
3. Chambers
4. You peel them

Mixed Bag #8
Page 283

1. Little by little
2. They are types of lifts
3. grasp
   revolve
   reach
4. 78. Add the numbers outside the brackets and multiply by 3 to get the number inside the brackets.

Mixed Bag #9
Page 285

1. track
   tree
   rink
2. You scrape them.
3. Spare
4. Going in style

Mixed Bag #10
Page 287

1. It's next to nothing
2. You set them
3. running
4. shapes

Mixed Bag #11
Page 289

1. about
   grain
   taint
2. Let down
3. You crack them
4. workman

Mixed Bag #12
Page 291

1. Lots of enthusiasm
2. You plant them
3. clock
   chat
   patch
4. **48**. 18 (+2), 20 (+4), 24 (+8), 32 (+16), **48**. You double the number added each time.

About the Author

Leslie Bendaly, speaker, workshop leader, and bestselling author, challenges and inspires organizations, teams and individuals to tap the best of themselves and provides them with the tools they need to realize their goals.

She is a North American leader in the fields of teamwork, group processes, synergistics and peak performance management in environments of change. Leslie is seen as a pioneer in the development of tools and systems for increasing synergy and exceptional performance within teams and across organizations as well as in identifying trends with which individuals and their organizations must be in tune if they are to continue to thrive. Her tools and concepts have been developed and tested through her work with hundreds of organizations from large multinationals such as IBM and Warner Lambert to government and small community organizations.

Her other books include *Strength in Numbers*, *Games Teams Play*, *More Games Teams Play*, Organization *2000*, *Winner Instinct* and *The Facilitation Skills Training Kit*. Leslie's work is recognized in *Who's Who in Canada*, *Who's Who in Canadian Business*, *and Who's Who of Canadian Women*. She is sought after as a facilitator of team development and planning processes.